Katharina Niciejewska

Dark Pools and Flash Trading

New trends in Equity Trading?

Anchor Academic
Publishing

Niciejewska, Katharina: Dark Pools and Flash Trading: New trends in Equity Trading?
Hamburg, Anchor Academic Publishing 2015

Buch-ISBN: 978-3-95489-365-2
PDF-eBook-ISBN: 978-3-95489-865-7
Druck/Herstellung: Anchor Academic Publishing, Hamburg, 2015

Bibliografische Information der Deutschen Nationalbibliothek:
Die Deutsche Nationalbibliothek verzeichnet diese Publikation in der Deutschen
Nationalbibliografie; detaillierte bibliografische Daten sind im Internet über
http://dnb.d-nb.de abrufbar.

Bibliographical Information of the German National Library:
The German National Library lists this publication in the German National Bibliography.
Detailed bibliographic data can be found at: http://dnb.d-nb.de

© Anchor Academic Publishing, Imprint der Diplomica Verlag GmbH
Hermannstal 119k, 22119 Hamburg
http://www.diplomica-verlag.de, Hamburg 2015
Printed in Germany

Contents

List of Figures VII

List of Tables VII

List of Abbreviations VIII

1. Introduction 1

2. Equity Trading and its new phenomenons – Definitions and Characteristics 3

   2.1 What is Equity Trading? 3

   2.2 Dark Pools – Definition 4

   2.3 Dark Pools – Rationale 5

   2.4 The Trading Framework 7

      2.4.1 Pre-trade phase 8

      2.4.2 Trade phase 8

      2.4.3 Post-trade phase 10

   2.5 Orders 11

      2.5.1 Market Orders 11

      2.5.2 Limit Orders 12

      2.5.3 Peg Orders 13

      2.5.4 Hybrid and Complex Orders 13

      2.5.5 Order Parameters 14

         2.5.5.1 Display Parameters 14

         2.5.5.2 Quantity Parameters 16

         2.5.5.3 Time in force Parameters 17

3. Different types of Market Structures and Market Liquidity 18

   3.1 Physical and electronic markets 18

   3.2 Continuous Markets 19

   3.3 Quote-driven and order-driven markets 19

   3.4 Displayed and nondisplayed markets 20

   3.5 Market Liquidity 20

      3.5.1 Block liquidity 21

      3.5.2 Supply and demand for liquidity 22

4. Pricing in the dark pool sector 24

4.1 Price discovery 25

4.2 Price derivation 28

5. Regulatory Framework and Control in Europe 30

5.1 Regulatory Framework in Europe – MiFID 30

5.2 Financial Regulation and Dark Pools 34

5.3 Reporting and transparency 35

6. The structure of dark pools 36

6.1 Exchange orders and brokers as sources of dark liquidity 37

6.2 Multilateral Trading Facilities (MTFs) as sources of dark liquidity 38

    6.2.1 Electronic limit order books 39

    6.2.2 Crossing Networks/Price Reference Systems 40

6.3 Broker desks as sources of dark liquidity 43

6.4 Direct market access (DMA) as source of dark liquidity 44

6.5 Hybrid business models as sources of dark liquidity 45

6.6 Market overview 46

6.7 Dark sector evolution 50

7. Trading in the dark 51

7.1 Execution issues 51

7.2 Trading Strategies 55

    7.2.1 Block Trading 55

    7.2.2 Program Trading 56

    7.2.3 Algorithms and Algorithmic Trading 56

    7.2.4 High Frequency Trading 59

    7.2.5 Gaming 63

7.3 Aspects of Technology 64

    7.3.1 Order Management Systems and Execution Management Systems 65

    7.3.2 Routing Engines 65

    7.3.3 Matching and Pricing Engine 67

    7.3.4 The FIX Protocol 67

8. Conclusion 69

List of References 73

List of Figures

Figure 1: Market Clearing Price 27

Figure 2. Daily market share equities (FT, Trading Room, 2012) 46

Figure 3. The Thirty-Millisecond Advantage, "The New York Times", 23.07.2009 60

Figure 4: Broadcom's Performance on the 15th July 2009, FAZ, 06.08.2009 62

List of Tables

Table 1. Fidessa Fragmentation Index, report for week ending 27th July 2012,
        Fidessa Group plc 53

List of Abbreviations

ATS	Alternative Trading Systems
BATS	Better Alternative Trading System
CESR	Committee of European Securities Regulators
EBBO	European Best Bid and Offer
ECN	Electronic Communications Network
FD	Fair Disclosure
IOI	Indicator of Interest
MiFID	Markets in Financial Instruments Directive
MTF	Multilateral Trading Facility
NASDAQ	National Association of Securities Dealers Automated Quotations
NBBO	National Best Bid and Offer
NMS	National Market System
NYSE	New York Stock Exchange
OHR	Order Handling Rules
OTC	Over-the-counter
SEC	United States Securities and Exchange Commission
SOR	Smart Order Routers

1. Introduction

The history of equity trading began hundreds of years ago, when the first companies needed money for their projects and asked private investors instead of banks for equity. Later, in 1969, when the first electronic stock trading was introduced in the U.S., namely Instinet or Institutional Networks, trading became electronic. Shortly thereafter, in 1971, the first fully automated exchange, the so called NASDAQ (National Association of Securities Dealers Automated Quotations), was created. The NYSE, which was founded as a physical, order-driven, auction-based market, entered the electronic sphere in the early 1970s. In 1977 the first electronic trading montage screen, showing quotes on NYSE stocks, went live through Instinet's efforts. Another pioneering platform was Investment Technology Group's (ITG) POSIT (Portfolio System for Institutional Trading), which was introduced in the late 1970s. POSIT was already crossing block trades electronically away from the exchanges on a scheduled basis (Domowitz et al, 2008: 1).

From 1980 on brokers started to use their own electronic proprietary trading systems to cross trades for clients. Further pioneering move was the introduction of the first after-hours crossing platform in 1986 by Instinet. In Europe it was the Paris Bourse (today part of NYSE Euronext), which developed a leading edge electronic trading platform for the French stock market as early as 1989. Although electronic trading developed during the late 1980s and early 1990s, it was only in the late 1990s and beginning of the 21st century that technology, communications and networking reached a state that ATSs became useable (ibid).

Although the concept of hiding is not a new concept, as it has been around for several years, in the form of hidden orders, the dark pool phenomenon and crossing network structure came into focus only in 2002, when the INET, a product of a merger between the Island ECN and Instinet, announced that it would stop displaying order book limit prices to avoid connecting to the relatively slow Intermarket Trading System (ITS). With this action INET effectively "went dark", as limit orders were no longer visible to market participants. A formal dark pool platform, Instinet CBX, followed in 2003 (Domowitz et al, 2008: 1).

While in 2003, 7 crossing networks has been established as providers of nondisplayed liquidity, only 5 years later their number had surpassed 40. Although estimations about the current dark volumes are not easy, as these volumes appear mixed with all OTC trades, it can be assumed that approximately 15 % of all traded volume in the U.S. and about 10 % of all European trades are executed in the dark. With this fast growth, in only one decade, electronic trading and especially dark trading became a very important market mechanism. This becomes even more apparent when looking at the projections which suggest that at least half of European and U.S. markets will trade in the dark within the next 5 years (Grant, 16.12.2009).

This book is supposed to give the reader a better understanding of equity trading in general, with a focus on new trading phenomenon's, namely dark pools and flash trading. It provides a definition of equity trading in general and dark pools in special in chapter 2 where these terms as well as other trading related terms are explained and an overview of the trading framework is given. Moreover the most important types of orders and order parameters are explained to the reader.

In order to better understand the concept of the new mechanisms, chapter 3 gives an overview of the different types of market structures and explains the importance of market liquidity. The chapter is concluded with a differentiation between liquidity suppliers and liquidity demanders.

In chapter 4 the pricing in the dark pool sector is explained. The importance of price discovery and price derivation is highlighted.

Chapter 5 deals with the important topic of regulation and control. Due to the multiplicity of different national regulations, the book focuses only on the European regulatory framework, which is MiFID.

Finally in chapter 6 the structure of dark pools is explained. All different sources of dark liquidity are highlighted and a market overview of the dark sector is given. The chapter is concluded with a regard on the dark sector evolution. Chapter 7 continues with the dark pool sector and focuses on the different trading strategies in this sector. In addition the technological aspects of dark trading are explained in non-technical terms.

Chapter 8 will summarize all important information about equity trading in general and dark pools and flash trading in special. Further some possible future trends for the industry development are drawn.

2. Equity Trading and its new phenomenons – Definitions and Characteristics

In the following chapter a basis about equity trading and dark pools should be given to the reader. The most important terms will be explained and an overview of the trading phases and the different types of orders and order parameters will be given.

2.1 What is Equity Trading?

In general equity trading can be described as the buying and selling of securities, which can take place on a regulated market, for instance at one of the major stock exchanges like the New York Stock Exchange (NYSE) or the London Stock Exchange (LSE), or off-exchange, bilaterally, on the so-called Over-The-Counter (OTC) markets.

Equity trading can be performed by the owner of the shares directly or by an agent authorized to buy and sell on behalf of the share's owner. Proprietary trading or principal trading is buying and selling for the trader's own profit or loss. In this case, the principal is the owner of the shares. While agency trading is buying and selling by an agent, usually a stock broker, on behalf of a client. Agents are paid a commission to the broker for performing the trade and for supplying the investors with research on shares. Stock exchanges and brokers have so called market makers who help to limit price variations (volatility) by buying and selling a particular company's shares on their own behalf or on behalf of others clients. They are called market makers as they influence with their trades, usually of huge blocks of shares, the price of a share. They buy certain shares because they assume that according to researches, news flows or the market situation, these shares give a very interesting buy opportunity and so they can sell them to investors. The blocks of shares are only kept for a short period of time, usually of maximum an hour (wikinvest).

2.2 Dark Pools – Definition

Having define equity trading, and before getting on a more detailed discussion on the subject, a common definition of the term dark pool should be given to the reader. Dark pools can be defined as a type of alternative trading systems (ATS) that do not display prices to the public, unlike on exchanges and other platforms with a "public order book", and which are often owned by big banks like Goldman Sachs and Credit Suisse (SEC Fact Sheet, 21.10.2009).

Another definition is given by Erik Banks, who defines a dark pool as "a venue or mechanism containing anonymous, non-displayed trading liquidity that is available for execution" (Erik Banks, 2010: 3).

He defines further that anonymous, non-displayed trading liquidity means order flow that is not visible in public order books, like those operated by exchanges, and that this fact leads to the name "dark" liquidity. Furthermore a venue is any electronic platform and a mechanism is any structure within an exchange or any participant in the market that offers non-displayed liquidity. Execution is, according to Erik Banks, the capability to trade an asset through the submission of an order (ibid).

Thus it can be summarized that a dark pool is an accumulation of orders to buy or sell stocks (or other assets), but whose existence is not publicly known or advertised.

According to his definition a dark pool resembles a traditional visible market in terms of structure, function and executing according to market rules, but differs as it indicates not the market depth.

2.3 Dark Pools – Rationale

Having said this in the following a look should be taken on why dark liquidity exists and why the number of dark pools and other mechanisms is growing in recent years.

In general new financial products or markets are always introduced in order to bring market participants advantages, like costs savings, higher returns or faster execution times. In the case of dark pools the primary drivers are confidentiality, reduced market impact, cost savings and price improvements. To explain these drivers a simple example can be used: If, for instance, an investor wants to buy a large number of a certain stock, he will try to do so by being as quietly and confidentially as possible, as if his intention becomes public there is a risk that other investors might try to jump ahead of the investor to buy the same stock. The price of the stock would increase in such a case. This would create an unfavorable price movement for the investor. Of course, this would not happen if the investor would try to buy only a small number of the stock, as a small order would not generate the same interest in the market. Thus only large trades, so called block trades, which are defined as those in excess of several thousand shares per trade, are central to dark liquidity (Banks, 2010: 5).

Another driver for trading in the dark is cost saving. In general it can be assumed, that all electronic trading generates cost savings, as all execution that is done off-exchange avoids the payment of exchange fees. In addition there is the possibility of price improvements, as active sell-side and sophisticated buy-side institutions use advanced technologies and analytics for different strategies, like high frequency trading or algorithmic trading. These strategies are designed to take advantage of electronic trading and to increase short-term returns. Venues that are able to take or provide liquidity away from conventional exchanges are important in this process and can attract buy- and sell-side investors. It can be considered that any mechanism or venue that brings together sellers and buyers in a confidential manner, reduces market impact, generates fees savings and creates the possibility for price improvements, will succeed. In the case of dark pools all four advantages are given, which helps to explain why their market share has increased in recent years (ibid).

Indeed various catalysts have led to the development of new venues in the last years. First of all technological innovation plays the most important role in the evolution of the off-exchange sector. Without the development of communications networks and the processing of speed and power, the creation of efficient and reliable platforms and sophisticated routers and algorithms, as well as rapid pricing and matching routines would have not been possible. Although a closer look at the technical aspects will follow later in the book, a correlation of the development of new venues with the rise of increasingly sophisticated technologies is obvious.

Further to the technological innovation regulatory changes have been fundamental to the development of the dark sector. Those changes came in various forms and across various jurisdictions, but the most important to mention include the Regulation on Order Handling Rules (Regulation OHR) in the U.S., the Regulation Alternative Trading Systems (Regulation ATS) in the U.S. and the Markets in Financial Instruments Directive (MiFID) in Europe. Another catalyst for the growth of the off-exchange market was the so-called decimalization, so the moving of the minimum quoted price to 0.01 from some larger amount, which had as consequence that smaller price increments led to lower spreads, which in consequence led to lower profit opportunities and this in return led to the reduced willingness to risk capital. Indeed the consequences of decimalization were quite dramatically as it has caused average trade size executed on exchanges to decrease by 70 % in the U.S. and by 50 % in Europe. As it became more difficult to cross block trades without being noticed, more business was routed to the non-visible markets (ibid: 15).

Further to the catalysts described above one other reason for the increasing importance of off-exchange trading rest to mention which is capital accumulation and mobility. Actually capital is a raw material of every economy, and includes the equity and debt obligations firms raise to fund their operations. Therefore as the global demand for goods and services has risen in the past, the demand for capital financing has risen as well. As industrialized and emerging nations continue to build on their economic bases it is quite likely that the amount of outstanding capital will continue to rise. And as capital is mainly supplied by institutional investors, like mutual funds, hedge funds, insurance companies, and other asset managers, this has radically reshaped capital mobilization, allocation and trading. The most important of these investors, namely hedge fund investors, are especially interested in sophisticated, high-volume trading strategies, like high frequency trading or program trading, and these are critically important to the electronic markets and dark trading. Of course, capital needs to be centralized in order to give interested parties the possibility to trade it in an efficient and effective way. Therefore both exchanges as well as over-the-counter venues are crucial for capital trading. But as the supply of capital has increased enormous in the last decades, any single venue is able to handle the large amount of outstanding capital on its own. Therefore there is a need for a multiplicity of venues, and this made it possible for new venues, including dark venues, to develop and expand. Further to the accumulation of capital also the ability to move capital quickly across markets had helped in the development of new platforms. Both traders and investors ask for rapid possibilities to buy and sell, or transfer capital, and as this demand will probably continue, one can assume that venues, which offer such services, will continue to benefit (ibid).

2.4 The Trading Framework

Investors trade for different purposes and over different time horizons. Therefore their demand for and supply of liquidity are very different. But although different trading strategies exist, the process of trading typically follows a logical sequence that represents an entire cycle. The key elements of any trading framework include three phases, which will be described in the following. These phases comprise together the "lifecycle" of a trade. Some of the steps described in the following, like the entry of a trade are very short, lasting no more than a few seconds or even milliseconds, while other steps such as the execution can last for milliseconds, seconds, minutes, hours or even days, depending on the specifics of a transaction. And still others such as clearing and settlement can take up to several days to conclude.

2.4.1 Pre-trade phase

The first step in the pre-trade phase is the analysis of potential trading opportunities. This analysis can occur through fundamental analysis, technical analysis, benchmarking, or other models. The output of this analysis process is the identification of a specific security that should be bought or sold. The second step of the pre-trade phase includes the analysis of the opportunity in relation to the current trading portfolio. As the addition of a single security can radically change the characteristics of a portfolio, it is critical to understand the effects before the execution of a trade. The last step in the pre-trade phase is the identification of specific transaction strategies. The trader must decide which venues should be triggered, when the trade should be executed, what prices are acceptable and so forth. Further the trader must also define a strategy for the case that an order cannot be filled immediately. He must decide whether the order should be canceled or rerouted in such a case. Another decision regards whether to display an order or to leave it in the dark. Each one of these points contributes to the development of a trading strategy (Bhowmik, 2012).

2.4.2 Trade phase

The first step in executing a strategy that has been developed by a trader during the first three stages of the trading framework is the order entry. Order entry is a positive action that must be taken by a trader. The trader can chose between various order entry mechanisms, like verbal/telephonic communication to a broker, or via direct input into some type of order application, like electronic communication networks (ECN) entry via interface (e.g. application program interface), broker algorithm via interface, and so forth. All these mechanisms are valid but whereas voice via broker is less common in today's marketplace, algorithms are increasingly common. In fact investors send less order flow to brokers because they can reduce costs and minimize the potential for information leakage by using flexible technologies for order entry by themselves. The order entry stage gives the trader the opportunity to define precisely what should be done with regard to the purchase or sale of securities. Numerous types of orders can be selected with parameters that define price, time, venue and so forth. While certain clients rely on voice-only orders which are typically taped in order to ensure accurate transcription of details and which may be followed by a confirming message from the broker, many other clients prefer to directly input their own orders electronically by supplying relevant details in the entry fields provided by the application. The more complex the order details, the greater the flexibility needed within the application. Of course, if a large number of orders should be entered, as in the case of high frequency trading for instance, the process must be automated. In such case batches of orders may be generated automatically by the trader's model and submitted either directly into the market or via a router to one or several brokers or venues (ibid).

The second step in the trade phase is order routing. Even though an order has been entered into an order management system or conveyed verbally to a broker it must still find its way to a marketplace. This step is heavily dependent on technology. The only practical way for tens of thousands of individual orders to enter into a marketplace at any one time is by placing them into an electronic line and leading them to a destination. This line is a network that connects the client terminals with the servers that feed the engines of a particular exchange. The faster this network connection and the more robust the server architecture and the closer to the physical proximity of an exchange, the quicker is the delivery and the execution. The client or the broker gives the instructions where the order should go. While some of the routing is very standardized and can be viewed as a simple set of instructions stating that the order should be moved from the order entry terminal and delivered to a particular destination, also more complex routers exist. These routers are known as smart order routers (SOR) or routing algorithms and they ensure that the order is treated in a very specific way if it is not filled immediately. In such cases the order can be moved sequentially through other random or defined dark of light venues in search of best execution opportunities (ibid).

The third step in the trade phase is finally the execution. This step is in fact completely technology-driven and based on pricing and matching routines that run in an automated way. As the loss of even some milliseconds in the process can be harmful to a trader's position, the most important factor in order execution is time. Therefore advanced technologies are employed, in order to route orders into venues, and to flow them through pricing and matching engines, which match and execute, or reroute orders, with a minimum of latency (ibid).

2.4.3 Post-trade phase

After an order has been executed, details must be reported to all stakeholders. This comprises the first step of the post-trade phase. Reports are sent to the trader, but also to regulatory bodies and to the market at large. But of course the levels of detail which are reported are not the same to all parties and also the time horizons over which reporting must occur are different. While deal confirmations are send out immediately, via an order management system or through electronic messaging, the reporting to the public or to regulators may occur at the end of the trading day or at some later date. Same as the execution of an order, also the reporting is largely driven by technology (ibid).

The last step in the trading lifecycle is the dual process of clearing and settlement. Once the trade has been executed and reported, it must pass through the clearing process, which is usually managed by an independent clearinghouse or the clearing department of the venue. Clearing includes the confirmation of all relevant details of the executed trade, including the counterparties, the price, the quantity and so forth. If any of these details do not match then the process is diverted to a resolution department where further investigation must be undertaken. After the clearing process is concluded the final stage can begin, namely the settlement. This step includes the delivery of cash for shares and vice versa, between the two parties to the trade through the clearing and settlement agent. This step is extremely automated and usually involves electronic debits and credits to the cash and securities accounts of buyers and sellers. Once this stage is completed the trade lifecycle is concluded (ibid).

2.5 Orders

In trading instructions are given how and when to buy and sell securities. These fundamental instructions for the transfer of liquidity are orders, and they are essential in creating and transferring liquidity. In the following the most common types of orders will be explained. Within the broad classes of orders certain additional parameters may be attached, to specify for example the speed of execution, to achieve price improvements, to limit the risk, or to determine the method of display.

Before describing in the following the major types of orders, some important terminologies in relation to order types should be defined:
- Bid: the highest price at which one party is willing to buy a security (representing the demand side of the transaction) (Deutsche Börse Glossary)
- Offer: the price at which one party will sell a security (Banks, 2010: 34)
- Best bid: the best buy offer. The highest price at which one party is willing to buy (www.centralact.com)
- Best offer: the best sell offer. The lowest price at which one party is willing to sell (ibid)
- Inside spread: the difference between the best bid and best offer (Banks, 2010: 34)

2.5.1 Market Orders

Market orders, alias unpriced orders, are the classic form of orders. They are not-limited buy or sell orders which should be executed as soon as possible, at the next price in the market.

Within the class of market orders several subtypes exist, including stop orders, trailing stop orders, market-to-limit orders, market-if-touched orders, market-on-close orders, market-on-open orders, uptick/downtick orders and sweep-to-fill orders.

The most used of these order types are stop orders, trailing stop orders, market-to-limit orders and sweep-to-fill orders (Deutsche Börse Group, 2009:11).

Stop orders are similar to limit orders: securities are sold or bought if a trigger price is attained. In the case of insufficient volume a fill cannot be guaranteed even if the stop is triggered and the order converts into a market order.

Trailing stop orders are similar to stop orders except that a trailing amount is attached that moves with the market price.

Market-to-limit orders are not limited buy or sell orders which should be executed at an action price or in the continuous trading at the best limit price in the order book. A Market-to-limit order is only accepted if there are only limit orders at the opposite site in the order book. If only a part execution of a market-to-limit order is possible, the rest of the order will be placed in the order book with the limit of the part execution (ibid).

Sweep-to-fill orders are orders that should be executed as fast as possible at the best available price, regardless of venue. That means that these orders are submitted to the first venue with the best price and are filled to the extent possible. Then the remaining portion sweeps to the next venue with the next best price, and so forth until the order is completed. Typically with each sweep the price becomes less favorable (Banks, 2010: 36).

2.5.2 Limit Orders

Further to market orders a limit can be added to an order. Limit orders are buy or sell orders with a price limit. They should be executed at a certain price or better. If the price limit is not reached, limit orders are not executed and depending on the investors instruction these orders are than deleted or the investor gives also a time limit, which indicates how long a limit order is valid. An unfilled limit order is placed in the exchange's limit order book for future execution. While in the process of being filled, a limit order is considered to be a working order.

Subtypes of limit orders are: stop limit orders, trailing stop limit orders, limit-if-touched orders, limit-on-close orders, limit-on-open orders, discretionary orders and intermarket sweep orders (Deutsche Börse Group, 2009: 11).

2.5.3 Peg Orders

Peg orders are based on a price that is pegged to a recognized base reference, such as the NBBO or the EBBO. Within the class of peg orders the following subtypes can be considered:

- Primary peg orders: are peg orders that peg to the same side of the base reference
- Market peg orders: are peg orders that peg to the opposite side of the base reference
- Midpoint peg orders: with midpoint orders the execution of an order takes place at the precise midpoint course between ask and bid price of the base reference. Midpoint orders interact only with other midpoint orders and not with the other orders in the order book.
- Alternative midpoint peg orders: are peg orders that peg to the "less aggressive" side of the midpoint (Interaktivbrokers.com).

2.5.4 Hybrid and Complex Orders

Further to the order types noted above, many other orders can be created, by combining different order types with each other. An example is for instance the cross order, which is an order to buy and an order to sell the same stock at a specific price. Sometimes broker receive an order from one customer to buy and from another customer an order to sell the same security; this is then a cross order, which is not fictitious.

The most complicated order types are called algorithms, which contain many different parameters that define precisely how an order is to be filled (Banks, 2010: 40).

2.5.5 Order Parameters

Many of the orders from the four main order classes' described above can be further defined through additional parameters, namely display parameters, quantity parameters and time in force parameters. In the following an overview over the most common parameters should be given.

2.5.5.1 Display Parameters

Display parameters need to be added specifically, with a "do not display" instruction. If such an instruction is not given, an order is assumed to be visible to the public in most marketplaces. A "do not display" inscription can be applied to all or only part of the order. If it applies to all of the order, the order is a hidden one, if it applies only to a part of the order; the order is an iceberg order. It should be noted at this at this point that both hidden and iceberg orders are critical to dark liquidity formation. Therefore a closer look at these two order types will be taken in the following.

2.5.5.1.1 Hidden Orders

Hidden orders are non-visible limit orders, which are embedded in a venue's dark book. Generally, they are excluded from the MiFID pre-trade transparency regulations, because of their huge volume compared with normal market size. In order to comply with MiFID requirements for orders which are large in scale the minimum size for a hidden order is specified in Table 2 in Annex II of the MiFID Implementing Regulation 1287/2006, titled "Orders large in scale compared with normal market size" (CESR, 2010: 18).

Hidden orders rest hidden, even if the rest volume of a part execution is smaller than the requested minimum size. Generally hidden orders are executed in the order book as limit orders, which mean that the execution follows the price-/time priority. However if there are hidden and visible orders at the same price, visible orders are executed before hidden orders (Deutsche Börse Group, 2009: 15).

2.5.5.1.2 Iceberg Orders

Iceberg orders (also known as reserve orders) are orders which make it possible to an investor to place orders with huge volume into the order book without making the whole volume visible to the public. Iceberg orders are limit orders with a defined total volume as well as a defined visible part of the order, the so called peak-volume. Both, the total volume as well as the peak-volume, have to match a so called round lot, which means that the volume of an iceberg order has to be a normal unit of trading for a security, which are generally 100 shares of a stock.

In the continuous trading when the first peak has been fully executed, another peak is automatically displayed in the order book. The hidden part of the order is then reduced by the corresponding number of shares. When an iceberg order's displayed part is fully executed, and the next peak converts from hidden to displayed status in the order book, the newly displayed peak also receives a new time stamp which determines its time priority (Banks, 2010: 42).

For instance, if the total volume of an iceberg order is 100,000 shares and the peak volume is defined as 10,000 shares, the market would see only 10,000 shares on the ask or bid side of the order book, depending whether the order would be a buy or a sell order. When the display quantity of 10,000 shares would be executed, the next peak volume would be automatically visible to the market, and wait for its next opportunity to get a fill. The trading system automatically displays new peaks after additional executions, until the final peak is displayed or the order is cancelled. As iceberg orders are not specially marked in the order book, it is not visible from the outside whether an order has a rest volume or not. Only after the full execution the total volume is visible.

But the immediate automatic display of a new peak after the currently displayed peak is executed creates a distinct pattern in the order book updates that is observable to any trader who monitors the order book closely. A trader who detects an iceberg order cannot determine the iceberg order's size although its peak size may provide a signal. But as peaks are executed and new ones are displayed, the trader can form more precise forecasts of the order's total size. So rather than disclose the information about the order size right away, iceberg orders sequentially reveal more information as peaks are executed. Iceberg orders are therefore often justified and promoted as an order type that facilitates the execution of large orders with minimal price impact, a property that should appeal to large liquidity traders. In the order book iceberg orders, including their hidden volume, have a higher priority than hidden orders (Deutsche Börse Group, 2009: 15).

Although both hidden and iceberg orders assume lower priority than visible orders that have the same price level, these order types are, according to recent empirical evidence about traders' order submission strategies on electronic limit order books, more and more used. The growing importance of these special types of orders can be seen in the fact that they make up recently around 44 percent of all Euronext volume (Buti et al, 2008: 3).

2.5.5.2 Quantity Parameters

In addition to display parameters, many of the orders described above may also contain quantity parameters. These parameters specify the action to be taken if the full order cannot be executed instantly. The most common quantity parameters are:

- Fill-or-kill (FOK): with this designation the order should be immediately and entirely executed. If this is not possible the order should be cancelled (Private Trader Club; Trader Lexikon).
- All-or-none (AON): with this designation the order should be immediately and entirely executed. If the execution of the entire amount is not possible the order remains in force pending future execution unless it is specifically cancelled. An

all-or-none order is similar to a fill-or-kill order, except that it stays in force until it is withdrawn (Interactivebrokers.de: 2012)

- Immediate-or-cancel (IOC): with this designation the order should be immediately and entirely executed. Any unfilled portion of the order is to be cancelled shortly after the order has been submitted (deifin.de: 2012).
- Minimum acceptable quantity (MAQ): with this designation at least a minimum amount out of the full order size must be filled. When an MAQ order is partially filled and the residual order size is lower than the MAQ, the MAQ will be reset to the residual order size (BATS Europe, Market Guide, 2012: 2).

2.5.5.3 Time in force Parameters

Further to display and quantity parameters some orders can also contain time in force parameters, which define certain duration limitations or order extensions. One of the most common of these time in force order limitations is the "Good-for-day" instruction, which indicates that the order is only valid for the current trading day, so until exchange closing. Other common time in force parameters are "Good till date", "Good till cancelled" and "Good after order" (Banks, 2010: 43).

The list of order types and order parameters described above is not complete. In fact many other subtypes of orders can be created. The main point to highlight at this point is that orders are key for market activities.

3. Different types of Market Structures and Market Liquidity

Further to the different order types described before also different types of markets exist. These apply to all kind of securities and assets, but this book will only concentrate on market structures which apply to stocks. The most common differentiations in market structures for stocks are: physical and electronic markets, continuous markets, quote-driven and order-driven markets as well as displayed and non-displayed markets.

The success of all of these markets relates on market liquidity and on the way in which that liquidity is accessed (dark or light). Therefore in the following also some aspects of liquidity should be explained to the reader.

3.1 Physical and electronic markets

Although the operation of a physical and an electronic market may be identical, the interactions of participants are quite different. While in an physical market traders, brokers, specialists and other exchange personnel negotiate on the physical trading floor in order to buy and sell stocks, in an electronic market these parties are in front of their monitors, usually in different places, and negotiate via advanced technologies.

Both structures have their advantages: while physical trading offers speed and immediacy that is simply not available via an electronic marketplace, which inevitably has a degree of latency, electronic trading gives access to participants from various locations, removes the human element from the trading process, and let therefore less room for errors. Finally electronic trading also offers possibilities for participation to a much larger number of buyers and sellers (Banks, 2010: 48).

The advantages of electronic markets explain why there are more and more of these. Indeed there are not many physical markets any more. These, that continue to have a physical trading floor, like the NYSE or the LSE, operate separate electronic markets of their own as a supplement to their physical activities (ibid).

For the topic of this book it is important to note at this state that the entire class of ATSs and MTFs, which is described later in the text, and which form a key part of the dark liquidity sector, represent an important part of the entire electronic market sector.

3.2 Continuous Markets

Further to a classification of markets by their physical or electronic existence, markets can also be described by their operating hours. The most common form of market structure in the financial sector is the continuous market. As the name suggests, in a continuous market trading is possible on an ongoing basis during the trading session, for instance from 9 am to 4 pm, or throughout the day, as it is the case for instance for some electronically traded securities, which can be traded 24/7 (Banks, 2010:49).

To complete the picture it should be mentioned that further to continuous markets also call and brokered markets exist. But as these forms are rather less common, they will be not further described in this book.

3.3 Quote-driven and order-driven markets

Markets can also be classified by their "motor". In this case one can distinguish between quote-driven and order-driven markets. While in a quote-driven market execution must generally be done through a market-maker or dealer, rather than via another trader or investor, in an order-driven market buyers and sellers are permitted to execute directly with each other, without the use of market-makers or dealers. Therefore prices of securities in an order-driven market are determined through the publication of buy and sell offers, which are conveyed via orders, while in a quote-driven market prices are determined through quotes supplied by market-makers or dealers, which they alone are allowed to adjust in relation to relative supply and demand (Banks, 2010: 220-221).

Indeed most of the global exchanges and ECNs are order-driven, though markets such as NASDAQ and the LSE are mainly quote-driven.

3.4 Displayed and nondisplayed markets

Markets can also be classified by the visibility. In a displayed market offers to trade are, at least to some point, visible to the public, while in a dark market offers to trade are, as the name suggests, not visible to the public. Nondisplayed markets are called dark markets, and are the subject of this book.

In fact there are many ways of transmitting orders that are not visible to the public. One can consider iceberg and hidden orders carried in limit order books as well as nondisplayed positions in agency orders held by brokers. Also dealer liquidity that is specifically not exposed or orders on the blotters of buy-side and sell-side proprietary desks and latent orders resting with passive, buy-side, investors are part of the non-displayed markets. Indeed one can find dark orders in all market structures described above, including exchanges, electronic limit order books, crossing networks and proprietary desks. Dark orders play an important role in trading, as much of the trading interest would stay unmatched without the possibility to submit orders in a nondisplayed way (Banks, 2010: 52).

After having described the different types of market structures it should be stressed out, that various subtypes exist, such as nondisplayed, electronic, quote-driven markets or displayed physical, order-driven markets.

3.5 Market Liquidity

In the past, especially in times of market stress, when investors became risk averse and moved to the sidelines, liquidity disappeared rapidly from the market. This shows, that liquidity is central to any efficient financial marketplace. During these periods markets became difficult to trade and the achievement of financial goals became complex and expensive. It was difficult to establish price transparency and to introduce price volatility. Therefore it is essential for any efficient market to have a steady supply of liquidity (Banks, 2010: 31).

3.5.1 Block liquidity

Although market liquidity includes all forms of liquidity, large and small trades, in the following a closer look should be taken on large trades, so called block trades, as these can have important impacts on markets and are therefore central to the dark liquidity.
In general block trades are defined as trades with several thousand of shares per trade, for instance 10,000 shares in the U.S., but a block trade can also be defined in terms of a percentage of the daily trading volume (Banks, 2010: 206).
The impact of block trades can be seen a simple example: if a trader shows interest in buying 10,000 shares of a stock (where 10,000 shares represent a relatively meaningful fraction of the day's trading activity), the price of the share will probably rise, as sellers will adjust their offers in order to reflect the large buying interest. The same will occur of course in reverse if the trader emerged as a seller of a block of shares, where the price would be negatively impacted. This direct market impact would be much smaller if the trader would be only interested in some hundreds of shares (ibid: 32).

This example shows that block trades can move the market price in an unfavorable manner and therefore create negative market impact. Therefore any investor that actively trades block trades will search for possibilities to hide his interest and so reduce the negative market impact. For doing so two mechanisms can be used: rather to chose an entire black mechanism or to break down a large trade into a number of smaller slices. Both can help to achieve a better execution price than an undisguised display in the market.
However certain algorithms can nowadays detect if a block trade is sliced into a number of different visible orders which are routed to multiple venues for execution. The same is true if an order is placed into a dark venue for execution this can be detected, as certain

algorithms look for dark blocks, which are routed from venue to venue, in order to be filled. Any of these actions may leave "digital fingerprints" that be used by swift operators. Further there is a tradeoff between speed of execution and possibility for information leakage: if a trade will be crossed as a matter of urgency exclusively in the light markets, this trade will create some amount of market impact, while a trade that is crossed strictly in the dark may take longer to fill but should have no market impact. Therefore visible liquidity provides opportunities for information leakage and thus market impact, while dark liquidity protects against that information leakage and thus minimize market impact. Further it can be stated that small orders create less market impact than block orders (ibid: 33).

But it should be mentioned that not all dark pools are "equally dark". Those who take order flow from a public source might leave some information, as a trail can be created in moving from the light to the dark. In fact in almost any venue some information leakage can appear from time to time, for instance if orders are routed from and to other pools. These pools are considered as "gray pools". However for traders and investors seeking or taking dark liquidity it is important to know whether a pool is really dark.

3.5.2 Supply and demand for liquidity

Measuring liquidity and the size of the nondisplayed market is difficult, for the same reason that leads investors to the market in the first instance: lack of transparency. Indeed some venues count liquidity as volume, even if there is no fill, while others count only trades which were actually crossed. Still others count as volume all orders that pass through the venue. These different measures produce different results.

In general market liquidity can be measured through four different parameters:

immediacy, which is the degree to which a trade can be executed in the current moment,

- breadth, which is the cost of completing a trade,
- depth, which is the amount of a trade that can be done at a particular price,
- resiliency, which is the degree to which the price of a security reverts to its previous level following a trade.

These parameters help to define the specific trading strategies that investors will take and will lead to the use of particular order types and venues (Banks, 2010: 55).

Furthermore it is important to note, within the discussion of liquidity, that there is an entire spectrum of liquidity suppliers and liquidity demanders: from those suppliers that are active and those demanders that seek immediacy, to those suppliers that are passive and those demanders that can afford to be patient. On the active side certain groups of trades can be found that regularly offer liquidity, to take advantage of liquidity demanding traders who are obliged to trade, because they face a high degree of immediacy. For instance market makers take advantage of liquidity-demanding traders, with the allocation of instant liquidity (ibid).

While market makers and demanders of immediate liquidity are on the active side of the liquidity spectrum, pension funds and other intuitional investors with a long-term horizon are passive investors. Actually passive investors have no plan to trade or will only trade if immediate traders will make it worthwhile. That's why they submit limit orders that are priced well beck of the market. If these orders will be executed the investors will win attractive profits and if not they will lost nothing.

In summary all the immediate and passive demand against active supply and passive supply interact to determine prices and flows in securities (ibid).

4. Pricing in the dark pool sector

Pricing and execution are essential components of the financial market and every financial product. If a market wants to survive it has to offer some economic benefit. The same is true for a transaction to be of use, it must be executed. It is of no use to submit orders that are not filled or are rerouted so often, that the speed advantage of the market is lost. Of course the same obtains within the dark pool sector where clients expect cost savings and orders to be filled efficiently.

In visible markets price discovery is the central activity. Although this is not necessarily true for dark markets it is however important to understand pricing in order to understand the whole business model, including all costs and benefits that affect all stakeholders of a business model. Especially these four types of costs and benefits are essential to understand:

- Benefits for providers (exchanges): depend on the employed business model – While in a classic business model a venue charges small fees on every trade (regardless of whether the client is posting or taking liquidity) plus annual fees and eventually also connection fees, in a rebate model a venue will pay rebates for those clients posting liquidity but will charge more for those taking liquidity.
- Costs for providers: usually cost structures with a significant fixed component and a smaller variable component. The fix costs are mostly technology investments while the variable costs relate to the amount that must be paid in rebates in order to attract liquidity plus technical and support resources. Of course every provider must ensure that all costs per share of execution remain below the revenues.
- Benefits for clients: primary cost saving from reduced market impact plus possibly rebates earned from posting liquidity.
- Costs for clients: execution costs plus commissions or spreads if a broker model is used. Clients using an ECN or crossing network may also pay a one-time or annual access fee (Banks, 2010: 94-96).

It should be noted at this point that costs for clients have markedly declined in the last years since the introduction of different new venues. This is especially true for traders dealing via crossing networks, ECNs or DMA. According to different studies trading through dark pools reduces costs in comparison with alternative venues. The Quantitative Services Group (QSG), for instance, has found that dark pool executions reduce market impact by 62 % (QSG, 2008). But trading in the dark has not only advantages for clients. Indeed studies have proven that trading on a non-visible basis has also economic benefits for providers of platforms. But of course providers of platforms need to see sufficient benefits in terms of market share in order to operate their business models. One research study has proven that the annual breakeven revenues need to be between €10 million and €20million in order to support a MTF. Based on estimations of costs and revenues, this corresponds to 5 % market share. Only few venues achieve this share (e.g. BATS Chi-X Europe). This calculation shows that a consolidation in the near future is very likely, as venues will try to gain sufficient market shares in order to work cost-efficient. But while new venues will have to fight for market shares, traditional exchanges will probably not enter into this price fights, as they are usually still having important market shares of their home markets (ibid).

4.1 Price discovery

All exchanges that are bringing together sellers and buyers serve as price discovery tools. And also other venues, like ELOBs for instance, can fill a similar role. Order books can be seen as warehouses for open orders that are waiting to be executed. While market orders can be usually executed immediately (if the security is liquid and the order book is balanced), various types of limit orders may need to be stored in the order book. For traders it is of big benefit to know what is stored in the order book. Therefore if a trader can distinguish the depth of orders, he is in a better position to execute at a better price (Banks, 2010: 97).

It can be distinguished between order-driven markets that feature only the best bid and best offer, known as "top of book", and those which show multiple prices in an open limit order book (LOB) which are known as "market by price". In a "market by price" model the depth of the market can be easily detected. While a deep market is characterized by a significant bid and offer volume together with a broad range of prices, a thin market has almost no bids and offers and if any those are only having a small range of prices. But no matter whether a market is deep or thin, the first priority in the queue for an order is price and the second priority is time. If two orders have the same price, the one submitted first will receive the first matching priority. Further to these two priorities other priority rules, like visibility and volume, may also exist but these are always ranked behind price and time (ibid: 98).

When orders enter a venue they are usually first ranked by price. Therefore on the top of the queue are those bids with the highest price and those offers with the lowest price. Secondly the venue applies the second priority rule which is mostly time. After this a venue may also apply its third priority rule, for instance display status, so a visible order may be ranked higher than a dark order. Finally a fourth rule might distinguish if small orders will be executed before big orders or the other way around. After the orders have been ranked, a matching engine determines which orders can be matched. The venue matches first the orders with the highest ranking: a buy and a sell order. If these orders do not have the same size usually a venue will fill the smaller order completely and then fill the rest of the larger order with the next highest order in the queue. This process continues through the queue until the point where bid and offer are identical. This is the last order that will be executed, as at the level below the buyers bid is below the sellers offer (ibid: 99).

Orders that can trade are priced usually by using one of the two common pricing rules. While in the single price auction all trades occur at the same market clearing price, in the continuous market an entering order should be immediately matched against its book.

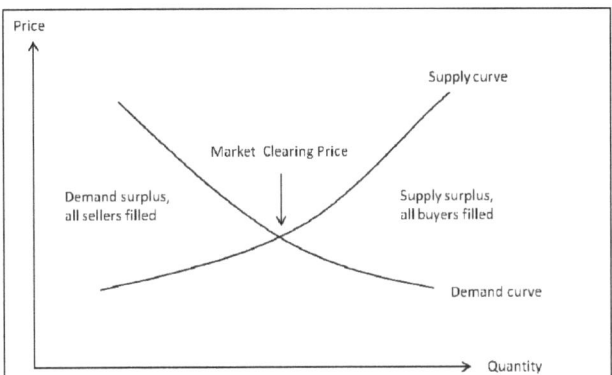

Figure 1: Market Clearing Price

As can be seen in the figure the market clearing price is the point where supply is equal to demand. Below the clearing price a demand surplus exists. In this case all sellers have their orders filled. While above the clearing price a supply surplus exists and all buyers have their orders filled.

In contrast to the single price market, a continuous market uses discriminatory pricing via an order book to fill open orders. As soon as a new order enters the market the matching engine tries to arrange an immediate match. Depending on the order type some orders are executed immediately (like market orders and very aggressive limit orders) while others must wait in the order book for a match (if the order is not an IOC or a FOK order). A match is done by the matching engine if a new order can be matched with the highest ranking order on the opposite side of the order book. If the volume of the new order is bigger than those of the highest ranking order, the rest volume will be matched with the next highest ranking order, and so forth (Banks, 2010: 101).

Both pricing methods have their advantages: while a single price auction produces maximum gains from trading, the continuous trading allows trading to occur at will and permits trading of a larger flow of orders as it is not limited to trading at a single price. In both of the cases the interaction of different order types (market orders, limited orders, dark and visible orders) at different prices leads to price discovery. The only case when dark orders do not lead to price discovery is, when they are executed in a crossing network with reference to a base price (ibid).

4.2 Price derivation

As crossing networks are not auction mechanisms but rather platforms to collect orders, they source prices from primary exchanges and match trades based on these reference prices. Therefore, as mentioned above, nondisplayed orders that are matched in crossing networks do not lead to price discovery. And also orders that are executed against a base reference price in any other venue do not contribute to price discovery. While in Europe dark pools can keep their anonymity by basing their prices on a reliable reference, like the EBBO for instance, and by doing so avoid the MiFID pre-trade data publication rules, in the U.S. venues usually execute dark orders against the midprice of the quoted market inside spread. Both approaches do not lead to price discovery, but are a form of price derivation. But this does not mean that all dark liquidity has no price impact. Indeed while trades executed via crossing networks might not be able to influence prices directly, iceberg and hidden orders executed on exchanges or ECNs can influence prices. This is so, as those orders interact with the visible part of the order book. For instance if a stock is bid at € 10 and offered at € 10,10 and a hidden bid exists at € 10,05, than a selling market order of € 10 will be executed at € 10,05. Without the hidden order the execution would have been at or below € 10. So the hidden bid has supported the market in this case and influenced the price (Banks, 2010: 105).

After have described the fundamental mechanisms of pricing an execution a closer look at the regulatory framework should be taken.

5. Regulatory Framework and Control in Europe

Regulation is for any well-running financial system. Indeed national markets that feature a strong regulatory framework are generally better placed to attract capital than those without such controls. Of course no regulatory regime is perfect and especially during times of financial crises regulatory missteps tend to be revealed. But in general, however, regulatory checks may be considered as effective and useful and are essential to the smooth conduct of financial business. In the following a look should be taken how the increasingly significant activity of dark pools is and should be regulated. More specifically a look at the financial regulation in the context of dark pools, the effects of regulatory changes on the development of dark pools, the optimal level of formal regulation and the potential opportunities for self regulation will be taken. All of these with focus on the European market.

5.1 Regulatory Framework in Europe – MiFID

Regulatory changes have been fundamental to the direct and indirect development of the dark sector. Such changes have various forms in different countries. While in the U.S. the Regulation OHR, Regulation ATS, Regulation NMS and the Regulation FD, among others, play an important role, in Europe it is the Markets in Financial Instruments Directive that plays a major role. In the framework of this book a closer look at the situation in Europe should be taken.

The Directive 2004/39/EC, also known as Markets in Financial Instruments Directive (MiFID), was implemented in the European Economic Area as part of the European Commission's Financial Services Action Plan, in November 2007, and replaces the former European financial law, the Investment Services Directive (ISD), which was introduced in Europe in 1995. The main aims of this European Union law are to provide harmonized regulation for investment services, and to increase consumer protection with increased competition between investment services providers. Although the regulation affects almost all investment services, especially the European equity trading was influenced by this law as the key aspects of MiFID are the client order handling, the pre-

and post-trade transparency, and best execution.

For client orders MiFID requires that they have to be executed by the investment companies in a prompt, fair and expeditious way. Although these requirements are widely similar to existing behavior of business rules, one new detail was added for client orders: the requirement to make pubic client limit orders that are not immediately executed. With this requirement venues should be bounded to consider the details of their client contracts and the venues they would use to make limit orders public (FSA Handbook, 2005: 12-13).

In addition to the regulation on client order handling further key aspects of the MiFID are the pre- and post trade transparency. This regulation has to be applied for trading in securities on the three main types of execution venues, which are regulated markets, multilateral trading facilities (MTFs) and OTC trading. Pre-trade transparency rules require that firms operation continuous order book trading systems make available for each security the five best price levels for both bids and offers, including number of shares and orders. For auction trading systems the indicative auction price and volume must be displayed, and for quote-driven markets the best bids and offers of market-makers must be indicated. However certain exceptions exist, namely for platforms that operate as price reference systems, platforms that formalize negotiated transactions, orders held in an order management facility and transactions that are "large in scale" (LIS). The latter are defined by certain criteria within MiFID. Also trades which should be dark have to have a minimum order size, which is based on the average daily turnover and market capitalization of a stock, as defined by the Committee of European Securities Regulators (FSA Handbook, 2005: 13-14).

The post-trade reporting requirements are imposed under various articles, for example article 25, 28, 30, 45, in MiFID. Post-trade transparency requires investment firms to publish basic data, like price, volume, time, customer ID, venue ID, transaction reference number and so forth, of all trades in listed shares, even if executed outside of regulated markets, unless certain requirements are met to allow for deferred publication. These information need to be published as close to real time as possible, within the three minutes of execution, with delays for large risk trades by up to 60 minutes. The post-trade reporting features two dimensions: daily transaction reporting to national regulators demonstrating MiFID compliance, and publication to the market. The information can be submitted to national regulators via, for example, third-party services. These services are offered by platforms like the Deutsche Börse, for instance (Banks, 2010: 175). Furthermore the best execution regulation is a central aspect of MiFID. Best execution is primarily attributable to price, though other factors such as speed and probability of execution may also play a role.

Maybe the most important feature of MiFID for purpose of this book is that member states no longer require execution of securities transactions on regulated markets or exchanges, under the so-called concentration rules. The result of this rule is the direct support for MTFs and for automated trading systems. A multilateral system like the MTF brings together buyers and sellers in an equitable manner and in accordance with rules promoted by MiFID. Following MiFID the development of various MTFs as competitors for existing exchanges in the delivery of liquidity and execution has already started. Some of these venues operate both: dark pools in parallel to their light books (Banks, 2010: 12).

In fact MiFID has given established exchanges such as Deutsche Börse or the LSE additional competition, causing them to reformulate their own business models. By late 2009 more than two dozen venues existed in Europe, proving dark liquidity. Although the idea behind was to create a competitive landscape where trades could be executed through various kinds of venues, rather than through exchanges only, the regulations served as a form of deregulation, sanctioning the establishment and expansion of ATSs and MTFs. Some of the effects were increased competition, lower costs, improved execution, reduced transparency and fragmented markets and trades. Although most of these effects were mainly positive, some, namely reduced transparency had also negative aspects. Transparency is a two-edged sword with the advantages of confidentiality and reduced market impact on the one hand, and the ignorance of what is occurring in the dark on the other hand. Especially during a period of crisis it may be difficult to be sure that best execution per MiFID is occurring, that settlements are proceeding properly, that no increased instances of fraud are occurring, and so forth. It is worth considering the impact of stress events on dark pool activity to determine whether the sector has the potential of becoming the next problem area, as special purposes entities and asset-backed securities earlier (Banks, 2010: 166).

Another visible change due to the support of so much competition and the advent of so many new platforms is sector and trade fragmentation. Traditional exchanges have lost market shares to new electronic competitors and have been forced to redesign their business models. Trade fragmentation has also appeared and breaking up large trades into smaller number of pieces has become standard operating practice for many traders, and it is a trend that is expected to continue. One example of this phenomenon is the trading composition on the LSE, which has changed dramatically since the regulatory changes. While in 1999 the average size of trades was GBP 63,020 and the number of trades was 5.3 million, the average size of trades decreased to GBP 14,908 and the number of trades increased to 134.1 million in 2008. Similar trends are apparent in other major exchanges, which shows that trade fragmentation is a well-established practice (ibid: 167).

As MiFID in Europe and other regulations in other parts of the world have created fundamental changes in the traded market, the question at hand is whether these regulatory changes have led to certain unintended consequences, and whether the new platforms have gained market share so rapidly that the full extent of their activities is not well understood or monitored by regulators, and an increased systemic risk might lurk below the surface. Indeed when MiFID was created, little or no attention was paid to algorithms, flash trading, high frequency trading and so forth. It is also quite apparent that while MiFID have rightly sought to spur competition in Europe, the sponsoring regulators must be somewhat surprised at the speed with which new venues have been created and old business models have been abandoned. Even if adding regulations for the sake of simply doing so is counterproductive and burdensome and can even destroy markets, avoiding helpful regulation most likely means waiting for a disaster to occur, as the history of financial markets has shown (ibid: 180).

5.2 Financial Regulation and Dark Pools

Although efforts at harmonization and consistency are in place in some areas, like the MiFID regulation for Europe, the reality is that a global "patchwork" of financial regulation continues to exist. The complexity of the regulatory landscape is a direct result of the complexity of the current financial markets. This makes it necessary to provide an appropriate degree of oversight related to different dimensions of the system. Such tasks are typically allocated to specific regulators with a degree of specialized knowledge and this result this "patchwork" of controls. In Germany for instance, multiple regulators govern pieces of the system, but no one the whole. But regardless of the approach, the main point to keep in mind is that national financial regulators have a responsibility and interest in ensuring that their financial systems operate properly and that all products and markets are controlled, while still giving them enough freedom to create innovation.

View the increased importance of the dark market, the issue to consider is whether the regulatory approach needs to change. Indeed the more misunderstood and complex the activity becomes, the more difficult becomes also the work of regulators. Though the efforts made by MiFID and other regulations on off-exchange trading, certain questions are still open:

- Do pre-trade and post-trade requirements adequately protect investors?
- Do trade-through rules function properly?
- Are economic incentives for rebates, liquidity fees and payment for order flow equitable, or were certain participants being disadvantaged?
- Is there a clear and sufficient picture of trades being executed in the dark?
- Does reported volume correspond with what regulators expect given overall market statistics?
- Is high frequency trading and algorithmic trading beneficial or harmful? (Banks, 2010: 169)

The answers of many of these and other questions are still unknown.

On the one hand if regulation becomes too restrictive, the dynamics of the sector might change and the advantages might disappear. But on the other hand if there is insufficient regulation and if there is an inadequate understanding of what platforms are doing, the potential of misuse might increase dramatically (ibid).

5.3 Reporting and transparency

Reporting and transparency are important aspects of security, especially in a sector which is still in the development phase, as a tradition of reporting might be not well established. This is true for the dark pool sector, which is still in the development phase and therefore transparency is still quite underdeveloped. In fact, in many jurisdictions there are no specific rules that require trade reporting to reflex dark execution. In the U.S. for instance dark pools have the report trades only as "non-exchange" but not as "dark". Industry standards would be important, but so far no single industry standard has emerged regarding reporting metrics. Therefore what a venue reports to an official facility may be different than what it reports on its website or in marketing documents for potential clients. Furthermore different reporting standards exist in different countries.

For instance, there are different ways in which activity in the dark space can be measured: some venues count all touched orders, which includes also orders that are routed through a pool but not matched, other pools count only matched orders, even if orders might be only partially matched. Furthermore some pools that report matched orders do so by double counting the volume, by counting both buy and sell orders that cross. In all of the cases confusion can arise. If for instance a buy order of 1000 shares of stock ABC is routed through a venue 1 but is not matches, this venue might count this volume as it has been touched. The same order might be routed to venue 2 and again stay unmatched, however venue 2 does not report touched volume. If the order is routed through venue 3 and is matched, it is possible that venue 3 counts both sides of the trade as volume. For each of these 1000 shares the three different venues report the following volumes:

-

- Venue 1: 1000 shares
- Venue 2: 0 shares
- Venue 3: 2000 shares

As shown in the example above, uniformity in reporting standards would help to have less confusion with relation to the dark sector (Banks, 2010: 171).

Indeed there is still no single combined regulatory standard regarding best metric. Proposals for future consistency focus on having regulators require standardized reporting metrics, identifying each specific print as a dark execution and include the top names being executed in each venue.

Another approach might also be a degree of self regulation that is adopting certain agreed "self-policing" standards and then ensuring adherence to such standards. Of course such self regulation is deemed to be an effective layer of control that supplements, rather than replaces, rules and regulations coming from a financial authority or regulator. Indeed the application of some degree of self-regulation in the dark markets has been posited by some participants as potential solution for reinforcing controls without exposing the detailed activities of individual platforms. In the U.S. for example an ATS can choose to register as a self-regulating organization (ibid: 179).

6. The structure of dark pools

As mentioned earlier, a dark pool is a venue or mechanism containing anonymous, non-displayed trading liquidity that is available for execution. Having said this in the following the key mechanisms or rather the potential sources of dark liquidity will be explained.

The main sources of dark liquidity are iceberg and hidden orders, alternative trading systems/multilateral trading facilities (including electronic limit order books and crossing networks) and broker desks.

The main point to keep in mind is that dark pools are not all equal, but differ in terms of business models and technologies. Clients can chose between those that offer full services versus those with discounted services, between those with full order management and those with execution only services, and so forth. Each platform provides clients with different levels of services in order to best match their requirements. But no matter what kind of business model a dark pool has, the main aspect is access to liquidity with a minimum of information leakage and price impact as well as capability for price improvement (Banks, 2010: 59).

6.1 Exchange orders and brokers as sources of dark liquidity

Exchange orders and specialist books are main potential sources of dark liquidity within the exchange structure.

In order to compete with the growing number of dark pools and other electronic players, most of the world's largest exchanges participate in the dark sector through iceberg and hidden orders. Although the concept of iceberg and hidden orders is not new, the importance of these order types has certainly grown in the last years. According to Euronext Paris, more than 40 % of all trading occurs via hidden orders (Euronext, 2012).

But exchanges do not only compete with dark platforms though iceberg and hidden orders. In fact they put effort into enhancing their specialist book capabilities in order to be competitive with the new platforms.

Specialists exist only in certain order-driven markets, such as NYSE Euronext or Deutsche Börse, and run each a "book" that contains orders of a particular sock, like for instance the Deutsche Bank book, the Daimler book, and so forth. They are obliged to quote two-way markets in specific stock and maintain an orderly market in those stocks under defined rules. The standard functions of specialists include showing best bids and offers (thus becoming market makers), acting as agents by placing electronically routed orders on behalf of clients, managing order books containing client limit orders and serving as principals by taking one side of a client trade against own inventory.

By managing the order flow passing through limit order books, specialists determinate which orders remain dark and which are made visible. Actually specialist books are an important source of dark liquidity.

Another source are floor brokers, which operate in a similar manner to that of specialists. They hold discretionary orders (which are always dark) and have a significant flexibility in when and how they expose and execute their orders (Banks, 2010: 62).

6.2 Multilateral Trading Facilities (MTFs) as sources of dark liquidity

The wide category of multilateral trading facilities (or alternative trading systems) includes electronic limit order books (ELOBs)/electronic communication networks (ECNs) and crossing networks, which are all important players in the dark pool space. But before getting deeper into this topic, some definitions should be given to the reader.

Since the introduction of MiFID in November 2007 the erstwhile ATS have been renamed as multilateral trading facilities (MTF). They are governed under the provisions of MiFID, just like traditional exchanges (wikinvest.com, 2012). These facilities are, just like regulated markets, multilateral. Multilateral means that multiple parties can input their selling and buying intentions into the system and a transaction is established between these parties when intentions match. They offer visible and dark liquidity or a combination of the two and act as price discoverers or price derivers. MTFs must be registered with the relevant national regulator and are defined under the EC Directive 2004/39/EC:

"Multilateral trading facility (MTF) means a multilateral system, operated by an investment firm or a market operator, which brings together multiple third-party buying and selling interests in financial instruments – in the system and in accordance with non-discretionary rules – in a way that results in a contract in accordance with the provisions of Title II." (European Union, 2004)

In the United States, where the expression ATS is still used, they are defined as SEC-approved non-exchange trading platforms. Rule 300(a) of the U.S. SEC's regulation provides the following legal definition of an ATS:

"Alternative trading system means any organization, association, person, group of persons, or system that constitutes, maintains, or provides a market place or facilities for bringing together purchasers and sellers of securities or for otherwise performing with respect to securities the functions commonly performed by a stock exchange within the meaning of § 240.3b-16 of this chapter; and that does not set rules governing the conduct of subscribers other than the conduct of such subscribers' trading on such organization, association, person, group of persons, or system; or discipline subscribers other than by exclusion from trading." (SEC, 2000, Regulation ATS)

Under these broad definitions one can find a variety of different venues, including electronic communications networks, electronic limit order books and crossing networks. Electronic communications networks (ECN) are a form of ATS which collect and match orders and execute trades with public quotes. They are defined under SEC Rule 600(b)(23) of Regulation NMS. Actually ECNs are similar to exchanges but operate like electronic broker. Any ECN must be registered as a broker or a self-regulated securities exchange (Banks, 2010: 63).

To the general class of ECNs electronic limit order books (ELOB) are counted among. These are off-exchange order books of limit and market orders which may be visible, dark or both. Another form of ATSs are crossing networks or price reference systems. They are defined under SEC rule 1998 as:

"A crossing system is, typically, one that allows participants to enter unpriced orders to buy and sell securities. Orders are crossed at specified times at a price derived from another market." (SEC, 1998)

Crossing networks match buy and sell orders electronically without routing them to other exchanges or displayed markets. The execution price is usually the midpoint of a market price.

With these definitions in mind, a closer look at ELOBs and crossing networks should be taken, as important sources of dark liquidity.

6.2.1 Electronic limit order books

ELOBs are a form of ECNs that operate as electronic "off-exchange exchanges". They post visible orders and sometimes also mange portfolios of hidden orders. In contrast to traditional exchanges ELOBs simply aggregate bids and offers flowing through their networks without a "middle man". ELOBs are a relatively new phenomenon to the financial markets, but they hold reasonable market shares and especially the introduction of MiFID gave boost to these platforms. One of these platforms is for instance Turquoise, which makes up over 4 % market share in the European equity trading (FT, Trading Room, 2012).

Traders using an ELOB post their prices and volumes anonymously and the only information that are displayed to the public are: the ticker, the bid and offer price and the quantity. If received orders cannot be executed immediately within an ELOB, they will be routed to a primary exchange. Therefore execution levels in ELOBs are at least as good as those on traditional exchanges (Banks, 2010: 66).

ELOBs offer a number of advantages to its clients, among others orders can be inputted directly by traders and become actionable, the delivery mechanisms are generally client-friendly and the latency is minimal. Although many ELOBs are primarily focused on smaller trades (especially as far as their visible operations are concerned) with their advantages, like their simultaneous handling of dark and light liquidity, and their participation in the price discovery process, ELOBs became an integral part of the trading landscape.

6.2.2 Crossing Networks/Price Reference Systems

As mentioned earlier, crossing networks (or price reference systems) are venues that aggregate and match orders as a pure agency function. Differences to ELOBs are:

- Crossing networks display no orders. Other than with ELOBs there is no "trading screen". Instead orders are matched anonymously, usually in relation to some base price (like the NBBO or EBBO). Thus crossing networks can be seen as a kind of processor that brings together orders with a focus on confidentiality.

- Some crossing networks allow a degree of price negotiation between sellers and buyers. This is structurally not possible through an ELOB. Although price improvements are possible, most transactions in crossing networks are executed with reference to NBBO or EBBO.
- While with ELOBs orders are generally matched on a continuous basis during the trading day and after market close, with crossing networks trades can be crossed either continuously or selectively during the trading day.
- While some crossing networks accept all trading sizes, others concentrate only on large transactions. ELOBs are open to all trading sizes.

Although crossing networks are quite new in the marketplace, they have become popular with institutional investors. According to market estimations approximately 90 % of large institutional money managers and approximately 60 % of small money managers have already used a crossing network (Banks, 2010: 68).

It is no surprise that crossing networks are especially popular with large institutional investors, after all these investors with their large block trades search for possibilities to execute these trades with minimal market impact, and as crossing networks operate exclusively in the dark, they provide real benefits to those seeking for confidentiality. Further to confidentiality clients of crossing networks also benefit from lower execution costs. Actually the cost advantages result from the additional competition that crossing networks have added to the market. But this competition is not only positive. It can also lead to market fragmentation, which can impact the formation of liquidity. In fact there is a fine line between having too few and too many competitors. If a venue has only a fractional amount of the available liquidity of a stock, then the chances to fill a client's order decline. And if the fill rates of a venue are not competitive, investors will not route their orders to this venue. Therefore the success of any single crossing network is based on its ability to attract liquidity (ibid: 69).

Different types of crossing networks exist and can be classified by their structure, by their functions or by their client focus.

From a structural perspective the following crossing networks exist:

- Independent crossing networks, which are independent from exchanges or other financial institutions, as they are held by public investors (e.g. Liquidnet)
- Broker crossing networks, which are owned and operated by brokers (e.g. Goldman Sachs' Sigma X)
- Exchange crossing networks, which are owned by major stock exchanges (e.g. BATS)
- Consortium crossing networks, which are owned by a number of partners, such as banks, brokers or exchanges (e.g. BIDS). They are managed by independent management teams.
- Aggregator crossing networks, which may be owned by a consortium or be independent (e.g. Pragma's OnePipe).

From a functional perspective the following subclasses can be distinguished:

- Negotiated crossing networks, that permit a degree of price negotiation between participants (e.g. Liquidnet)
- Continuous crossing networks, that accept confidential orders and cross them on a continuous basis (e.g. Pipeline)
- Call market crossing networks, that accept confidential orders and hold them until a call auction is declared
- Block crossing networks, that target institutional sized blocks, and which are the major subclass of crossing networks (ibid: 71).

All of the crossing networks mentioned above can target a certain client group:

- Buy -side only, permits only the participation to large financial institutions, like hedge funds, mutual funds pension funds, and so forth. From an order flow perspective, buy-side flow can come from DMA, algorithmic trading, high frequency trading and program or block trading. An example of such a model is Liquidnet.

- Sell-side only, permits only the participation to financial institutions that serve buy-side clients, like banks, brokers and securities companies.
- Buy-side and sell-side, is the most common form of crossing networks. Examples in this category like POSIT or Pipeline, net liquidity from brokers and from buy-side investment firms.

Many of the above described crossing networks have relationships with other venues, so that they can provide access to additional liquidity to their clients. Furthermore the key strength of crossing networks is their flexibility, as specific types of crossing networks can be combined.

6.3 Broker desks as sources of dark liquidity

Broker desks or systematic internalizers are defined under the EC Directive 2004/39/EC: "Systematic internaliser means an investment firm which, on an organized, frequent and systematic basis, deals on own account by executing client orders outside a regulated market or an MTF" (European Union, 2004).

They are operated by the world's biggest banks and securities firms and play an important role in the dark liquidity area. Broker desks developed very robust institutional mechanisms for capturing valuable internal flows from either client orders passing through the firm or proprietary trading activities or both. Some of the biggest players in this sector created internal crossing systems to gather and match such flows. For example Goldman Sachs' Sigma X or Credit Suisse's Cross Finder, among others, began as purely internal crossing efforts.

Large banks and fund companies, like Merrill Lynch or UBS, feature large retail networks that generate a large amount of order flow which can be routed internally for crossing.

Those desks that are not part of such a firm with a large retail network usually have arrangements with third-party brokers related to the routing of customer order flow. As all of the crosses occur within a firm's book and orders need not to be routed to other venues, the activity of broker desks reduces transparency. However in addition to internal crossings, some of the largest brokers have also established their own dedicated crossing networks. Many also use algorithms, which have the potential of linking to other dark pools and generating additional dark liquidity. Such algorithms have been central to the rise of dark liquidity (Banks 2010: 76).

6.4 Direct market access (DMA) as source of dark liquidity

Direct market access (DMA) is an electronic facility that allows direct order flow from the trader into a light or dark market, without the intervention of an intermediary (e.g. a broker). Main users of DMA are buy-side investors with a certain degree of market knowledge, a relatively high degree of portfolio activity, and investors who trade large blocks. DMA is linked to smart order routers and algorithms, and gives therefore these users the ability to execute directly into an exchange or dark pool. This reduces transaction costs and latency and eliminates errors form "worked" orders. If an order is in a visible or dark book and a trader using DMA enters an order at the same price or better, the order is automatically matched. The control of order management and execution is in the hands of the trader (Banks, 2010: 78).

According to the research firm Celent, DMA market share in the U.S. is just below 20 % and in Europe it is approximately 15 %, while further growth is expected in the near future, and the need for faster execution and compliance in response to MiFID regulations are expected to contribute to this DMA growth in Europe. (Celent reports, 2008).

Although DMA is not a dark pool mechanism itself, as it does not create or house dark liquidity, it is indeed a mechanism that allows tapping into dark (and visible) pools, and therefore must be considered as a part of the marketplace.

6.5 Hybrid business models as sources of dark liquidity

While traditional exchanges, ELOBs and crossing networks match customer flow against customer flow, broker desks match proprietary flow against customer flow. But these are not the only possible combinations. In fact in the last years the boundaries of different business models have expanded significantly as participants have created hybrid business models. Therefore institutions wishing to act as sponsors of dark liquidity are using more and more multiple channels. A global stock exchange for instance, can participate in the dark liquidity sector through multiple mechanisms:

- Through hidden and/or iceberg orders
- Through an ELOB, which is owned by the exchange and that offers hidden and/or iceberg orders
- Through the exchange's floor brokers, that cross trades within their books before posting them out to the market
- Through crossing networks, which are owned by the exchange

With these multiple solutions exchanges can increase their share of crosses, and therefore attract more liquidity.

Of course many other hybrid models can exist and can help institutions to gain market share (Banks, 2010: 78).

6.6 Market overview

As per today already more than half of all European equities are already traded away from regular markets and the tendency is growing (Fidessa Group).
Therefore it is worth it to take a closer look at who are the players in this landscape.

Although the dark landscape changes in a continuous way, in the following a brief overview should be given about the most important venues which offer dark liquidity. Of course, as there are about 143 MTFs in Europe and within over 20 dark pools (and more than 40 dark pools in the U.S.) a complete list of all these venues is not possible at this point. The aim is however to show the variety of options that are available to traders (SEC Fact Sheet, 21.10.2009).

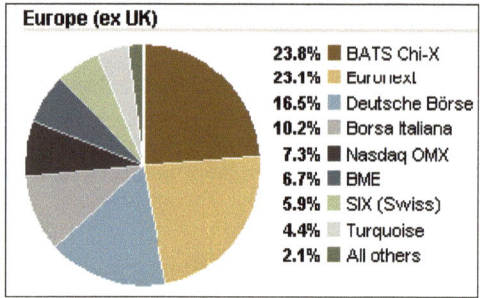

Figure 2. Daily market share equities (FT, Trading Room, 2012)

As can be seen in the figure above the most important venue in the European trading landscape is BATS Chi-X Europe Ltd, with a market share of 23.8%. Initially the two venues BATS Europe and Chi-X Europe were two separate entities, until in February 2011 BATS Global Markets bought Chi-X Europe for $300 million. Before the merger BATS was ranked as number 10 within the European market players while Chi-X was number 3 (Bremser, Schäder, FT, 2012).

BATS stands for "Better Alternative Trading System" and was founded in 2005 in the U.S. by several large banks, including Citigroup, Credit Suisse, Deutsche Bank, Lehman Brothers and Merrill Lynch. By 2010, BATS Europe was the second-largest MTF, behind Chi-X Europe, lading to it acquiring Chi-X Europe. All executions in the BATS order book are at the midpoint of the relevant base price, while orders can be placed in a dark book or in an integrated book that features visible and dark trades.

Chi-X Europe was established in 2007 by Nomura, BNP Paribas, Credit Suisse, Fortis, Goldman Sachs, Morgan Stanley and UBS, among others. Chi-X Europe was the first MTF that launched in anticipation of the European Union's November 2007 MiFID regulation, which paved the way for the introduction of alternative trading venues in Europe. With its registration as MTF by the Financial Services Authority (FSA) Chi-X Europe meets the same level of regulatory standards as traditional exchanges and receives the same level of supervision. Chi-X Europe's strategy is a low cost model, with execution costs of 0.05bps (based on a passive/aggressive ratio of 50:50). Chi-X MTF offers over 900 of the most liquid stocks across 20 indices in 14 European markets, in addition to ETFs and ETCs, all via both a visible order book and the so-called Chi-Delta non-displayed order book. Further Chi-X Europe offers various services to its clients, among others:
- Chi-Delta non-displayed book: this dark order book is a continuously matching order book that supports mid peg matching and uses the Primary Best Bid and Offer (PBBO) as a source of reference prices.
- Chi-Vision smart liquidity consolidator: which is able to source liquidity from the Chi-X visible order book, Chi-Delta non-displayed order book as well as from external liquidity providers (ELPs) using the so called Smart Order Routing technology.
- Sponsored Access: this service allows a firm (the "Sponsored Client") to directly connect to Chi-X using the membership of another firm (the "Sponsoring Firm" or "Sponsor"). The Sponsored Client is able to fully access Chi-X Europe's throughput, low latency trading engine and utilizes Chi-X's innovative order types.
- Off-exchange trade reporting: which includes several reporting services, like a delayed publication for block trades for instance.

47

- Chi-X Historical DataService: This provides access to Chi-X Europe historical tick and order book data, including the ability to rebuild full depth of order books from August 2008 onwards. The DataService also includes integrated search, analytics, custom report generation and data query services.

- Co-location & Cross Connectivity: this enables the participants to reduce their latency trading by co-locating their trading equipment in the same facility as the Chi-X matching engine (Chi-X Europe website, 2012).

The biggest competitors of BATS Chi-X Europe are Euronext and Deutsche Börse. Deutsche Börse is the primary German stock exchange and operates Europe's largest conventional visible platform by market value. Deutsche Börse participates in the dark space through its dark pool Xetra MidPoint, a dark platform for crossing blocks. Orders are executed at midpoint between the best bid and ask price of the open Xetra order book. Different to other European exchanges, Deutsch Börse so far is not shareholder in any MTF consortium neither owns a own MTF. In February 2012 the European Commission blocked the merger with NYSE Euronext, citing the fact that the merged company would have a near monopoly (Deutsche Börse website, 2012).

NYSE Euronext is a result of the NYSE / Euronext merger in 2007. The global exchange operates multiple dark mechanisms, including iceberg orders and working orders with its specialists and floor brokers. Also hidden order books and crossing networks in both Europe and the U.S. are operated by NYSE Euronext. Further NYSE Euronext is partner in BIDS Trading, a continuous dark block crossing network, and operates the NY Block Exchange (NYBX) joint venture with BIDS, a platform which matches dark orders against light, iceberg or hidden orders from the NYSE order book. NYSE Arca, the exchange's electronic trading platform, accepts light and dark liquidity and includes in its routing algorithm trading interest from participating venues. Dark orders that are not matched on Arca are routed to participating dark pool partners. With this business model Arca is one of the most successful dark venues in the U.S. with a market share of more than 14 % in equities turnover. Further the exchange operates NYSE Matchpoint, the exchange's U.S. crossing network, and SmartPool, a dark European MTF (NYSE Euronext website, 2012).

Another established MTF is Turquoise. Turquoise was created in 2008, by nine major investment banks: BNP Paribas, Citigroup, Credit Suisse, Deutsche Bank, Goldman Sachs, Merrill Lynch, Morgan Stanley, Société Générale and UBS. In the meantime Turquoise is majority owned by the London Stock Exchange Group (LSEG). Turquoise operates a MTF with two dark trading platforms; one for cash equities and another for derivatives. The Turquoise midpoint dark order book, coverts some 2,000 securities from over 19 countries, including all major European markets. The Turquoise integrated order book combines visible and dark orders, while trades in the Turquoise midpoint dark order book are executed at the midpoint of the European bid-ask spread (Turquoise website, 2012).

When it comes to pure dark liquidity Citigroup's platform Citi Match has the biggest dark pool for European securities with an average daily turnover in October 2010 of €327 millions. Client orders can rest within Citi Match via an algorithm to await the maximum available pricing improvement. Citi Match has advanced anti-gaming logic that insulates client orders against opportunistic orders (Citi website, 2010).

The second largest dark pool for European securities is Credit Suisse's CrossFinder. CrossFinder matched an average of 151 million shares a day (single counted), of which 13 million comprised blocks, according to Dmitri Galinov, director of Credit Suisse Advanced Execution Services (AES). Overall, CrossFinder is the largest U.S. equity dark pool, followed by Goldman Sachs' Sigma X, which trades 118 million shares a day (Schmerken, Advanced Trading, 2010).

These two dark pools have more than quadrupled their trading volume in only three years, to now more than 9 % of all U.S. equity volume (Mehta, 2010).

At the end of this subchapter it is important to note that the listing of MTFs and dark pools should be simply representative and not exhaustive.

6.7 Dark sector evolution

While in 2002 there have only been 10 dark pools in the United States today over 17 % of trades are done off the exchange, in around 40 licensed dark pools. In Europe the evolution is quite similar with approximately 33 dark pools that account for about 5 % to 10 % of European equity volume. This reflects a jump of almost fivefold in the period of time from January to October 2009 in Europe, and corresponds to around € 9.5 billion value of trades carried out within dark pools in compared to only € 2.2 billion in January 2009 (Grant, 02.11.2009). In the U.S. some 100 to 300 million shares per day are traded through some of the largest dark U.S. platforms (SEC Fact Sheet, 21.10.2009). And this evolution will continue due to the technological flexibility, the confidentiality and the cost saving possibilities that dark pools deliver to its clients. But while expansion in the dark market share will certainly continue, expansion in the number of dark venues has certainly reached a limit. Actually it is quite possible that the trial phase of business models and the period of proliferation of dark pools are ending. In the future business models will thus have to differentiate themselves from competitors to acquire a critical mass.

All of the business models described earlier have complex relationships between each other. For instance traditional exchanges can trade dark liquidity through any or all of the venues described before but they still rely on brokers who will push volume through their venues. While brokers for their part may be willing to support exchanges, but are operating or participating in crossing networks at the same time. Meanwhile a large bank might be a partner and a competitor of an exchange at the same time, by operating its own crossing network, and being partner with the exchange in another dark venue.

As mentioned earlier, the number of dark venues has reached a limit. Therefore it is no surprise that the competition within the new venues has become very aggressive. While established banks and exchanges ignored the efforts of the pioneering MTFs in the early part of the millennium, nowadays they have perceived the scope of opportunities and have placed significant resources into the development of platforms and relationships that can help them to gain back market shares and improve execution rates. On the other hand there are independent firms, sometimes backed with private equity capital, who are trying to serve niches of their own in order to satisfy their clients and stakeholders, but without getting in direct competition with the large players. Of course if the number of venues grows the chance of an order to flow into a certain exchange declines. That means that exchanges must be prepared to capture trades closer to the source (Banks, 2010: 87).

Therefore venues have developed different strategies to differentiate themselves. While some promote their high execution rates and the speed of execution others advertise the linkage to other platforms or their geographic reach. Whether all these efforts will help them to overcome the competition and the inevitable consolidation remains to be seen.

7. Trading in the dark

The decision to trade in the dark sphere rather than in the light sector is done by traders due to several considerations. In the following the most important issues related to execution in the dark should be focused. Further an overview of the key trading mechanisms and strategies should be given.

7.1 Execution issues

A trade can only be executed in the dark after it has been placed into a venue in some form. From the traders perspective this can occur in several ways. For instance the order can be directly routed to a crossing network or it can be routed to an exchange or ELOB as an iceberg or a hidden order. From a venue's perspective orders can be received via various channels, like for instance through DMA, broker routing or algorithm routing. In all of the cases: once the order is within the dark venue it stands ready for execution.

In the selection of the right way to execute a non-visible order a trader needs to consider several things, particularly the execution rates, the fungibility, the fragmentation and the information leakage. Execution rates can be defined as the number of shares entering into a venue that are matched. The execution rate of a venue is its benchmark to measure the venue's success. The better execution rates a venue has the more liquidity will be attracted, leading to increased possibilities of matching and execution, which in turn increases market share and attracts more liquidity, and so forth. On the other hand venues with low execution rates risk to be removed from smart order routers and routing algorithms, which leads to even less flow and lower execution rates, and so forth (Banks, 2010: 107).

Another important issue to consider whether to execute a dark order in a certain way is the fungibility of execution. Investors want usually efficient and price-competitive fulfillment of their orders. This indicates three things: venues at the lowest cost will likely have success, venues with a reliable pool of liquidity will attract more liquidity and venues with differentiated additional services may find opportunities to attract additional clients. In each of the three cases an increase of execution rates is likely (ibid).

Further to the fungibility of execution the fragmentation, so the splitting of a market into submarkets plays a role in the choice of a dark pool. It is quite common, that a security is traded in various submarkets simultaneously: on a primary exchange, which is usually the original listing market, on one or several regional exchanges, through the third market and via crossing networks. Fragmentation arises for a number of reasons, but very often a market is fragmented in order to serve different client needs. Not every client requires the same services. For instance the needs of an active day trader are different to these of a passive long-term investor or a block trader. While the one seeks speed of execution and immediacy, best price or large block anonymity might be most important for the other. In any of these cases, a venue that offers a focused client service is welcome, which leads to some degree of market fragmentation (Banks, 2010: 109).

Another reason for fragmentation is competitive profit opportunities. As technologies become cheaper, the entry barriers for new platforms are lower, so a bank or an exchange or a private company can enter the market without having enormous capital resources. Of course whether these new platforms can have enduring success depend in large part on their ability to gather and maintain a minimum amount of liquidity (ibid).

Last also regulatory encouragements can influence fragmentation. Indeed frameworks such as MiFID allow the creation of alternative venues. With their legitimization of alternative trading venues regulators encourage banks, exchanges and others to create their own platforms. This leads to various different pools (ibid).

Measuring fragmentation is not easy and depends on the availability of data and the consistency of definitions. The Fidessa Group has developed an index, the Fidessa Fragmentation Index (FFI), to measure the degree to which trading is occurring in multiple locations. The calculation is the inverse of the sum of the squares of market shares of each trading venue. The result is a coefficient that indicates how much fragmentation is occurring within a stock and across entire markets. A FFI coefficient of 1 means that all trading occurs within one single venue, usually the primary exchange. A FFI between 1 and 2 means increasing fragmentation. And a FFI above 2 means that trading no longer occurs in one single venue.

The following table reflects a sample of European and American exchanges during July 2012. It shows especially high fragmentation for stocks listed on U.S. exchanges. For instance, for the best execution of an order listed in the Dow Jones it was necessary to visit 5.1 venues, for an order listed in the DAX it was only necessary to visit lest than 2 venues to achieve best execution (Alternative Trading Systems Directory, 2010).

Weekly FFI

Index	FFI
Dow Jones	5.10
S&P 500	4.73
NASDAQ 100	4.09
FTSE 100	2.36
CAC40	1.96
DAX	1.96

Table 1. Fidessa Fragmentation Index, report for week ending 27th July 2012, Fidessa Group plc.

It is necessary to note at this point that fragmentation can be both: positive and negative. On the positive side fragmentation provides for competition. As venues are competing for order flow clients can profit from lower costs. Another positive factor is that clients can deal more closely with pools that match their own characteristics and aims. On the negative side fragmentation can lead to worse execution if orders are routed to the wrong pool.

Further to fragmentation also the information leakage plays a role in the selection of the right way to execute a non-visible order. A trader who submits an order ideally wants to direct it to a single venue and have it crossed entirely to eliminate any chance of information leakage. This issue concerns especially large block orders, as these can move market prices. Although a block can be crossed in a dark block network, sufficient liquidity may not be available. Therefore the order must wait until contra liquidity enters the venue or a more dynamic process must be employed such as breaking up the order into smaller pieces. If the order is braked up into smaller pieces the first fill is done at the best price and each subsequent fill deteriorates as liquidity is exhausted. However the average of the fills should be still more favorable than the single large block fill with its market impact. In general information leakage is more likely to occur in a setting where one or more participants stand to benefit at the expense of other participants such as day traders for instance which may have ways of interpreting information from a given pool. Therefore it is essential to understand the profile of a given pool. If for instance an unfilled portion is cancelled immediately, there is no risk of information leakage, as the unfilled portion is not routed to any other pool. If a trade is routed to multiple pools via algorithms, the cost impact needs to be considered and the likelihood of at least some information leakage increases. As the unfilled portions might be routed to several pools the time to complete the order rises and as execution time increases costs increase as well, according to some studies. In general friction costs appear to increase as an order is routed by algorithms to different pools, and therefore it can be supposed that these friction costs can be attributed to information leakage (Banks, 2010: 113).

Next to the execution issues described above in the following a closer look at the types of trading strategies should be taken.

7.2 Trading Strategies

Both the visible and the dark markets must be seen as a compendium of individual, sometimes competing, trading strategies. Performance of these strategies is dependent among others on the market: while a quiet and thinly market might favor certain approaches, a fast market with heavy volume may favor others. Market players need to adjust their trading strategies accordingly in order to be successful. They also consider whereas strategies can be executed most efficient in the visible markets, in the dark markets or in the combination of the two.

In the following an overview over the most common trading strategies should be given. These include block trading, program trading, algorithmic trading, high frequency trading and gaming. Not all of these strategies are exclusive to the dark sector, but they constitute the backbone of trading activity in this sector.

7.2.1 Block Trading

A lot of volumes in the dark pool sector come from block trading – either in pure form or as pieces of small orders. Venues offer two different models for block crossing: systems dedicated to block crossing, where clients can find contra-liquidity through submission of orders, and full service platforms which give access to multiple liquidity sources through a single entry point. The second model favors the sliced order approach.

The key reasons why dark pools present the best solution for block trades are confidentiality and the reduction of market impact. However, even if the decision is taken to execute the order in the dark sector, the trader must still decide whether to execute a block entirely or slice the block into many orders. The decision will be made on the basis of the price, depending on whether the price concessions demanded in dealing through a block dealer or submitting through a block crossing network or into a pool of latent liquidity are bigger or smaller than the price obtained by slicing the order into many smaller pieces. Whichever decision is made, the goal is to match buyer and seller away from the visible market in order to achieve a better price (Banks, 2010: 121).

7.2.2 Program Trading

A program trade can be defined as a single trade comprised of a portfolio of stocks, which is developed through a proprietary model and executed electronically. Instead of selecting individual shares, the program trade creates a portfolio of dozens or hundreds of shares and executes them as a package. Some exchanges have more precise definitions of what constitutes a program trade. The NYSE Euronext for instance defines a program trade as one with more than 15 stocks and $1 million market value. Program trading is becoming more and more popular in both visible and dark markets. For instance in 2009 the NYSE reported approximately 30 % of market share in the form of program trades. Program trading can determine both: optimal trading size and optimal trading location. With this approach program trading can create an entire list of orders and execute them en masse. This is a fast and efficient way especially for large portfolios. And as these portfolios demand for anonymity the dark pool sector is the ultimate place for program trading (ibid: 122).

7.2.3 Algorithms and Algorithmic Trading

Algorithmic trading can be defined as any form of trading that uses computerized processes to determine when, where and how to execute transactions in the marketplace. Algorithmic trading and algorithms allow for anonymity, efficiency, control and benchmarking and are therefore central to all types of institutional trading. Especially hedge funds, investment funds, pension funds and others use algorithms in order to reduce risk, take greater control of the execution process and to execute arbitrage and benchmarking strategies. According to market studies 25-30 % of US and European trading volume is handled through algorithms.

Algorithmic trading users can create very specific definitional parameters related to location, where to execute the order, routing, where to transfer the order if immediate execution is not possible, quantity, price, time and so forth. Further the rules can be customized to the specific needs of users. But algorithms are not only related to dark liquidity, they are also used in the visible market. While some of the most popular algorithms have focused on the search for hidden liquidity, others are acting as liquidity aggregators and try to find the best liquidity/price combination. The design of a typical algorithm is such that searches continuously for liquidity at the best possible price regardless of the location (ibid: 125).

Although the form of algorithms differs depending on the tasks of an algorithm, their structure has always the same key points. Indeed speed and accuracy are absolutely essential for the success of algorithms, as they must compete in a fast moving, competitive market against other algorithms, high frequency trading, large program trades and so forth.

A fairly standard algorithm slices up orders and routes each piece for execution using volume weighted average price (VWAP). Such an algorithm uses order generation logic, order placement logic and router logic to take a parent order slice it up into various child orders and route them to appropriate venues. The order generation logic includes mathematical instructions that determine how a parent order is to be parceled into separate child orders for individual execution. The order placement logic includes mathematical instructions that indicate how each individual child order should be executed. And the router logic includes mathematical instructions that indicate where each individual child order should be placed. This may include the instruction to spread the order across as many venues as possible (ibid: 126).

The structure of an algorithm depends on the goal it is intended to fulfill. While some goals are easy to achieve, others are much more complicated. Some key algorithm parameters include price sensitivity, horizon, predictability, confidentiality, immediacy, need to finish, tolerance and passivity. Depending on these parameters the complexity of an algorithm can be very high (ibid).

Many classes of algorithms have been developed by major banks, like Credit Suisse, UBS, Citibank or Goldman Sachs. Providing a complete list of all algorithms would go beyond the scope of this book, but some of these algorithm types are by now so common that certain investors use them as benchmarks:

- Time Weighted Average Price (TWAP): this algorithm works orders over time against a linear volume distribution.
- Volume Weighted Average Price (VWAP): this algorithm works orders over time by spreading trades along historical volume distribution.
- Flexible: this algorithm adapts its generation, placement or routing logic in response to the execution experience gained from previous child orders. These algorithms are extremely sophisticated as they can adjust tactically in order to improve the execution success.
- Implementation shortfall: this algorithm attempts to create an optimized trading plan that minimizes the difference between the decision price (or arrival price) and the final execution price.

These are only some examples of a long list of common algorithms. The most advanced algorithms are those which are able to adapt their logic in response to current events, such as breaking financial data or other market-sensitive news, and redirect their execution efforts accordingly. The decision which algorithm to use for a specific goal will made a buy-side trader in dependency on costs, speed of execution and performance. Although algorithms have improved efficiencies and may prove to be very profitable mechanisms, one should keep in mind that they also remove from the equation the intuition of traders with regard to market conditions and opportunities (Banks, 2010: 129).

Algorithms can also be used for benchmarking purposes. This makes them popular for investment managers that are measured against a specific metric. For many years benchmarking versus broad indexes or specific sectors has been common within the investment sector, but the advent of algorithms has facilitated the process. To define a specific target benchmark an investor can employ an algorithm that is designed to replicate the parameters associated with that benchmark and then allow it to execute per specific logic. Further to common market references VWAP and TWAP are also forms of benchmarks. The implementation shortfall is another very common benchmarking algorithm, which measures the distance between the pre-trade decision price and the actual price. It is also an effective way of gauging effectiveness over any defined implementation time-horizon, like for instance over 1 hour or 1 full trading day. Usually the creation of a benchmark is done in the pre-trade phase. During the pre-trade analysis the benchmark goal is defined and the costs are estimated. Also the acceptability of deviation away from the benchmark is defined during this phase (ibid: 130).

In summary the main advantages of algorithms are the creation of lower costs (in comparison to worked orders), the increased efficiency, the possibility of real-time execution monitoring, the possibility of access to multiple venues, the creation of flexibility through a large number of choices, the guaranty of anonymity in the market and the creation of a neutral benchmark indicator to track performance. On the other hand the disadvantages of algorithms are their possibility of increased gaming or information leakage, the creation of fragmentation, the delivery of average price execution at best, the possibility to miss on large blocks and, in the case of passive algorithms, the difficulty to react to rapidly changing markets (ibid: 131).

7.2.4 High Frequency Trading

The term high frequency trading is beside the term dark pool often mentioned in the daily financial media. But one need to be aware of the exact meaning of this term as there are several similar concepts, like flash trading, algorithmic trading and others, which can be easily mixed up in this context. For this reason a clear definition and description of the various terms in the high frequency trading context will be given in the following.

The basic idea of high frequency trading is to use very fast computers and algorithms to make use of market movements faster than competitors. In detail high frequency trading is a form of automated, tick-by-tick, high-turnover trading that is based on real-time data analysis and fast execution times. This form of trading is more and more common in both exchange and off-exchange trading, and according to the financial services company, Raymond James & Associates, high frequency trading strategies account for around 70 % of the U.S. daily market turnover and about 40 % of all daily market turnover in Europe (Bloomberg, 17.09.2009).

High frequency trading can occur in both: the visible and the dark market. The key to success of high frequency trading is high execution speed and resulting low latency. Indeed if execution cannot be guaranteed to occur within a particular window of time, usually measured in milliseconds, than it is of little use. Since high frequency trading requires access to real-time tick data, the demands on technology platforms increase substantially. A liquid stock generates for example between 2000 and 3000 tick changes per minute. One can imagine how data handling, data storage, computing speed and connectivity are paramount, if considering that this type of data requirement is needed for fully trading days and for various stocks (Banks, 2010: 132).

The following figure shows how the fast computer systems and algorithms give an advantage to investors which pay fees for the access to high frequency trading.

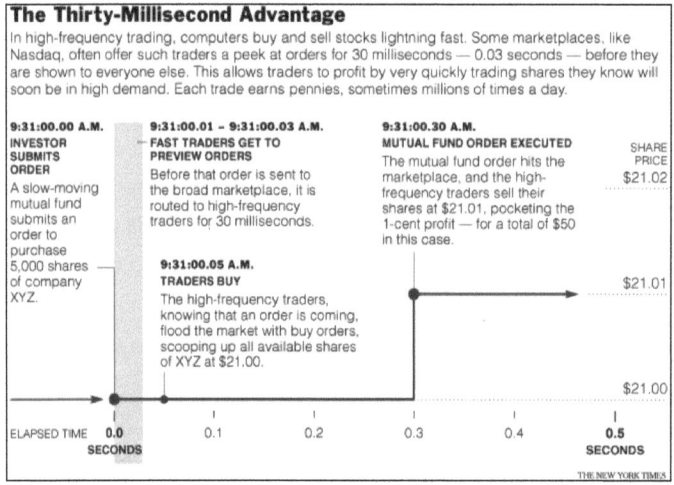

Figure 3. The Thirty-Millisecond Advantage, "The New York Times", 23.07.2009

In this example given by the New York Times a mutual fund, with a slow moving computer system, wants to buy 5,000 shares of a company XYZ. The mutual fund places the buy order in the system at 9:31 am. The gray zone in the figure indicates the next step: the order is not shown to all market participants but it is shown only to high frequency traders for 30 milliseconds. These fast traders know now that there is a buy order for 5,000 shares of the XYZ company coming from the mutual fund. With this information they buy all available shares of the XYZ company to resell them only some milliseconds later to the mutual fund with a one cent profit per share. In this example the high frequency traders gain only $50 but if one imagine this happens a million times a day one can also imagine how it comes that according to estimations high frequency traders generated about $21 billion in profits in 2008 (Der Aktionär, 10.08.2009).

Another real life example, which is often used in the daily media in order to illustrate the impact of high frequency trading, is the performance of the company Broadcom on the 15th July 2009. Broadcom is a semiconductor company listed in the NASDAQ. In the evening hours of July 14th Intel, the computer chip giant and a competitor of Broadcom, reported solid second-quarter results. According to an investor at a major Wall Street company who spoke to the New York Times anonymity, some investors saw an opportunity for Broadcom in these good Intel results and started to buy Broadcom directly after market opening on July 15th. But instead of buying large blocks at once and risk that Broadcom's price would go up institutional investors splited their orders into small pieces.

As can be seen in the following figure the shares of Broadcom started at $26.20 this day. When the traders using slower trading systems started to issue buy orders, these where not shown to all sellers at the same time. Instead some high frequency traders could see these buy orders 30 milliseconds before, as so-called flash orders. By seeing the buy orders 0.03 seconds before slower traders, the high frequency computers began to buying Broadcom before their slower colleagues, and could resell them at a higher price. These boosted the price of Broadcom as can be seen in the following figure.

Figure 4: Broadcom's Performance on the 15th July 2009, FAZ, 06.08.2009

As the price began to rise, the automatic high frequency programs began to issuing and cancelling undersized orders within milliseconds in order to find out the limit of the slower traders. With this technique they found out that the upper limit of slower investors was $26.40. The price rose to $26.39 and high frequency traders began to sell thousands of shares.

At the end of the day slower traders paid $1.4 million for a package of around 56,000 Broadcom shares. This was $7,800 more than high frequency traders. In total research firms estimate that high-frequency traders generated profits amounting to $21 billion in the last year with such deals (Duhigg, NYTimes.com, 24.07.2009).

The practice described in the example above mentioned the controversial flash pricing, where a pool "flashes" the price of a security on its books for several milliseconds before exposing it to the market at large. This window is sufficient for the most high frequency traders to make relevant trading decisions. However flash orders make up only a small percentage within all high frequency trading according to industry estimates. Due to its controversial character some venues banned flash trading. NASDAQ OMX, BATS and the NYSE Euronext, for instance, have already prohibited flash orders, while Direct Edge, for example, is still offering them (Kisling, Westbrook, 18.09.2009).

Beside the above illustrated examples there are also other high frequency trading strategies. Sometimes fast traders send out a stream of probing quotes to find out how much an investor is willing to pay for a certain share. The stream of probing quotes is sent out and quick cancelled until they cause a response. With this information the fast traders sell or buy these shares before the investor and offer them to the investor only a trickle of a second later for a small advantage. One further high frequency tactic is the so- called "piggybacking" on sharp price movements. This increases the volatility which increases the value of options held by traders (ibid).

ll these strategies have an unbelievable speed in common: high frequency traders are able to carry out up to 1,000 traders per second (The Economist, 30.07.2009). The NYSE Euronext for instance offers their clients order processing systems which allow execution in 5 milliseconds. This is a fast evolution in comparison to 2008 when execution took 105 milliseconds or 2007 when it took 350 milliseconds to execute an order, but it is still slow in comparison to NASDAQ OMX and BATS, which offer even faster times (Banks, 2010: 131).

7.2.5 Gaming

While most of the dark strategies are beneficial to market participants, there are also aspects about trading in the dark, which might present certain dangers, especially for traders and investors who are inexperienced or unaware. In the following a look should be taken at players and tools that search in dark pools for profit opportunities, at the expense of unsophisticated market participants.
One of these players is the so-called shark or fisher. These are individuals or institutions that search for distinctive strategies that were used in the dark. With this information they front run or position themselves to profit. This is done through algorithms that are designed to identify particular trading patterns and behaviors, or to detect dark trades. Some of the sharks are able to identify certain "styles" of broker algorithms. With this information they position themselves on the other side of the trade and take full advantage of the "digital fingerprint" left by specific broker algorithms. These methods

are not illegal but are of course not appreciated by neutral or passive market participants. Although these methods can also occur in the visible markets they are more used in the dark sphere.

Another common way for fishers to take advantage of activity in the dark is called gaming. This technique detects the presence of large orders in a pool and then profit form that knowledge by the right positioning of orders. As these methods can cost a venue's clients money, many venues impose certain antigaming controls in order to keep their clients. Such antigaming controls can take various forms. For instance some venues feature minimum execution size, which limits the ability for sharks to submit small ping orders in order to search for large blocks. Other venues block IOC orders, which are common for pinging a site. Of course this means that legitimate IOC orders cannot pass into the pool, but this seems to be an acceptable tradeoff for some pools. Another antigaming control can be the analysis of trading patterns in order to determinate if there is potential gaming activity occurring (Banks, 2010: 134).

All the strategies described above are not, apart from gaming, unique to dark pools. Regardless of the specific strategy, it is obvious that a great volume of liquidity is traded in the dark sector and any block trade, program trade or algorithmic strategy that fails to capitalize on such pools of liquidity might miss profit opportunities.

7.3 Aspects of Technology

The technology and architecture used in the dark sector is critical to the success of any single venue and of the market at large. Although a detailed discussion of all parameters that are important for the success of a venue, like reliability, access, speed, security, flexibility, network and data capacity, would be beyond the scope of this book, the central point is that if a venue cannot deliver to its clients such standards, any try to build a business platform risk to fail. In the following the essential dimensions of technology and architecture that touch both the user and the provider of dark venues, will be explained in "nontechnical" terms. Although not all of the components are exclusive to dark trading, this summary of the essential components should help to comprehend dark trading.

7.3.1 Order Management Systems and Execution Management Systems

Order Management Systems (OMS) and Execution Management Systems (EMS) are software- or hardware-based platforms designed to manage order entry, routing, execution and management of transactions. They serve as the centerpiece of advanced electronic and human market interaction. They can be seen as virtually standard for any active player, as they can simplify the entire process of complex order types, execution venues or algorithms.

OMS can be described as order manager and post-trade administrative manager, and is useful for active trading management. Whereas EMS is an execution application that is made for complex trading, high frequency trading and for arbitrage strategies.

Some of the core features of most OMSs include direct connectivity to brokers, exchange floors, ECNs and other ATSs, typically through a protocol such as FIX, real-time order management via on-screen blotter, detailed monitoring and review of open orders and other trading details, access to a suite of standard or broker algorithms, and post-trade support and reporting. The core features of EMSs are direct connectivity, real-time order management capabilities, algorithmic access, and advanced execution functionalities, such as customizable execution routines and real-time execution monitoring in support of complex trading strategies. Regardless of the specific features, OMS and EMS are used by traders to improve connectivity and execution response times, lower trading and execution costs, increase operational efficiencies and manage complex access points (Banks, 2010: 144).

7.3.2 Routing Engines

If an order remains unfilled, three choices remain: the order can be cancelled, it can remain resting in the order book, or it can be rerouted to another venue. As execution rates are still lower in dark markets than in the visible ones, order routing is very common in the dark space. Routing strategies are quite flexible and can be adapted to client requirements in order to gain best price execution and to minimize price impact and information leakage. For instance a router might take orders and route them to its dark liquidity partners for potential price improvements, or the order might be routed to an ELOB and to dark liquidity partners simultaneously, or to the financial institution's internal book and then to its pool partners, and so forth.

If, for instance, an order should be sequentially routed into a number of different dark pools to gain the best execution price in the shortest possible time frame, without resting in a pool to wait for contra-liquidity, until the order is filled, the steps involved in the routing process would be the following:

1. Step: Denote all relevant definitional parameters, like bid or ask price, number of shares, routing method
2. Step: Define the sequential logic of the routing method. This step includes the following phases:
   a. Define a "ping sequence" that indicates the sequence of multiple routing paths (for instance: which dark pools will be approached)
   b. Place the order within an automated order router that is capable of managing multiple routing paths
   c. Route the order to a dark pool in the "ping sequence" as an IOC order
   d. Reduce the outstanding number of remaining shares by amount filled in c., receiving back from the current dark pool the results of the IOC
   e. Check the number of remaining shares left in the order
   f. Revert to c. with the next dark pool in the "ping sequence" and repeat the process, verifying that the order is still marketable.

These are only the main characteristics of the routing process. Of course a real routing process includes much more information and is more complex than the steps described above (Banks, 2010: 149).

7.3.3 Matching and Pricing Engine

The matching and pricing engine can be described as the "brain" of any electronic platform. Its tasks are the evaluation of entering orders, rejection of orders which do not meet specific criteria, and comparison of already existing orders from the order book in order to determine if a match is possible. Such matching engines can be found in all dark and light mechanisms, including exchanges, ELOBs and crossing networks. In the first instance the venue must receive an order and place it in a matching book accessible by the matching engine. In most cases orders are submitted and received by common messaging, such as the FIX Protocol. First the matching engine screens for acceptable order types to make sure they conform to specified criteria, rejecting via return message to the submitting party any not conform order. For instance the engine might only accept displayed and nondisplayed market, limit and peg orders, plus those with IOC ad FOK designations, and reject all others before any attempt to match is even made. Once the screening is complete, any order submitted and accepted is regarded as firm, which means that the submitting party is obliged to delivery money or shares if the order is matched. Once the order is accepted in the engine, it is allocated by ticker into a separate subprocess dedicated to handling other orders with the same ticker. At this point the price contained in the order is compared with standing limit orders in the ELOB's sub-book for the share and a matching decision is made. If orders, whether dark or light, can influence the price, the engine will make an allocation based on the bids and offers of the orders (Banks, 2010: 152).

7.3.4 The FIX Protocol

The Financial Information Exchange (FIX) Protocol has become an industry standard for messaging and communications within the trading sector. According to estimations, 80 % of all massaging in the trading sector relies on FIX.

The FIX network connectivity from an application or OMS/EMS to a venue and vice versa can occur via a lease line, a wide-area network, such as the internet, a point-to-point virtual private network (VPN) or a hub and spoke setup.

The FIX engine is a software module allowing an application, OMS/EMS or a venue to perform a variety of functions, including managing network connections, creating and parsing in and out messages in a consistent manner and storing and recovering essential data.

The Messaging is of course at the heart of FIX and the common communication language is essential for rapid transmission and interpretation of all manner of messages. Many different types of messages exist, but for certain orders, like for indications of interest, single orders, day/multi-day orders, order modify/cancel requests, order cancel rejects, questioned trade and "don't know trade" and order status requests, standard message types exist. These common types of communicating contribute to rapid execution, which is essential to electronic trading (Banks, 2010: 155).

In general it can be said that the success of dark pools is the result of advances in technology and architecture. In the coming years, as technology will be improved, it is likely that processes will become even more efficient and more cost effective.

8. Conclusion

As the book has shown there are very good reasons why dark pools and other trading strategies, like flash trading, exist. The main advantages of these venues are, based on the discussion in the book, their confidentiality, which helps to protect large blocks of stocks from market exposure and so reduce the risk of market impact. Further they offer attractive execution fees, make use of smart order routing mechanisms in order to increase the speed of execution, and increase the chances of matching by interacting with visible and dark markets. However the book has also shown that the new platforms and strategies have not only advantages. In fact, dark pools can lead to bad fills if information leakage is not halted, they can lead to bad fills from gaming, and they can create confusion due to a multiplicity of venues, business models, and restrictions. Further they can absorb liquidity from markets responsible for price discovery, which may lead to questions about the solidity of a security's price. Finally nobody can predict so far what will occur during times of market crisis or dislocation, which creates a certain degree of confusion and uncertainty.

But although dark pools and other new mechanisms are not perfect the benefits that they can provide seem strong enough to outweigh any particular problems. This can be seen in their volume figures, which demonstrate increasing market share moving into the new venues, and away from traditional exchanges. Actually dark pools & co. have already overcome the phase of "prove itself" and are already a permanent part of the sector, which is reflected in a market share of 15%-20% of all trading activity in global equities. This figure reflects a jump of almost fivefold in the period of time from January to October 2009 in Europe. Whether this trend will continue in the years to come will depend on several factors. One of the main factors is the question whether the migration of market share from light to dark will continue. As the reduction or elimination of market impact is a very powerful motivation to trade in the dark sector, it is quite certain that the trend of migration from light to dark will continue. By various market estimates,

European and U.S. dark trading is expected to account for more than 50 % of all turnover by 2013 to 2014. Whether these predictions will be reached or not is somewhat irrelevant. What is for sure is that global capital and wealth is going to accumulate and therefore the investment process becomes increasingly focused on both efficiencies and execution without impact, both of which can be achieved via dark trading. The trend can also be seen in the fact that every major visible marketplace also operates separate dark channels, as mentioned earlier. For instance exchanges like the NYSE, the Deutsche Börse, or the LSE, have recognized the inevitability of the tilt toward dark execution, and have moved into the dark space. But this does not mean that the visible markets will disappear from one day to another. On the contrary: the visible markets support the price discovery process which is essential for the dark sector. Though even if fill rates begin to favor dark venues, it can be supposed that dark and visible markets will coexist over the medium term.

Another future trend to be considered is the increasing consolidation across existing pools. Indeed there is little reason to believe that the marketplace can support such a large number of venues. Even global exchanges like the NYSE and Euronext have merged with one another, in order to overcome the strong competition. In fact, the process of consolidation is already underway, as the strongest individual platforms seek to develop a larger market presence and as the weaker players give way by selling out. One other future aspect which has been discussed in this book is the growing sophistication and use of algorithms. Algorithms have been instrumental in supporting electronic trading and are surely a permanent part of the market landscape. This trend is likely to continue as sell-side financial investors, sophisticated buy-side entities and technology advisory firms continue to push the frontier of algorithmic trading. In fact, advances in algorithms must be seen as part of the trading "technology arms race". Venues and institutions that can deliver the best intellectual resources and investments in order to develop the "next generation" of trading will win this race. But one thing should be not ignored at this point: currently thousands of different algorithms exist. And although having choices is beneficial, there is also a natural saturation point, after which it becomes difficult to reasonably evaluate all of the available options. Algorithms are part of the quality versus quantity tradeoff, where any single high-performance algorithm is more valuable than dozens of mediocre ones. The risk with this trend is that the development of new algorithms will continue in a faster way than investors can evaluate and select them.

Furthermore the speed in processing and in execution times will play an important role in the future development of the marketplace. The world of electronic trading is build upon processing and execution, and therefore venues that provide the fastest speed are in a better position. Best execution rules, declared by regulators, point out that price is the top priority, but also make reference to the need for fast execution times. Therefore financial institutions and technology firms have invested large amounts of capital in the creation of engines with the ability to process and execute in a fraction of milliseconds or even microseconds. If hedge funds or high frequency trading funds, which seek maximum execution speed for their trading strategies, cannot be assured of the fastest execution in their preferred venue, they may redirect their flows elsewhere. In a business where volume trumps margin, capturing as much of this flow as possible is essential. Therefore it can be assumed that hundreds of millions of dollars will be spend in the coming years to continue shaving more microseconds off the time required to analyze, route, match, and execute.

Finally further regulatory enhancements will play an important role in the future development of the sector. As described in the book regulations like MiFID have helped a lot to the development of dark venues. For the future it remains to see if regulators might reverse themselves at some point, bringing dark trading back into the light. But although almost every day one can find news about a possible ban of dark pools and flash trading in the financial media, it seems unlikely that these strategies will be abolished, as long as no significant, widespread, and continuing problems like client discrimination on best execution, or large instances of outright fraud, or significant liquidity dislocations during the next major market crisis, will occur.

In the end it will be the needs of investors and traders that will decide on the future development of dark pools and other new trading strategies and venues. For the time being dark venues help them to execute their transactions confidentially, efficiently, and cost-effectively. If this should change one day, traders will surely no longer support the sector. On the other hand if these venues will continue to deliver the best technologies, create the most flexible business models and adhere to sensible regulations that promote confidence and security, it may be expected that they will continue to be an important and growing part of the market in the future.

List of References

A-Team Group (2010): Alternative Trading Systems Directory,
http://www.scribd.com/doc/40398731/Alternative-Trading-Systems-Directory-2010-1
(01.12.2010)

Banks, Erik (2010): Dark Pools – The Structure and Future of Off-Exchange Trading
and Liquidity, Palgrave Macmillan, 2010

BATS Europe (2012): Market Guide,
http://www.batstrading.co.uk/resources/participant_resources/BATSEuro_MarketGuide.p
df (01.08.2012)

Bhowmik, Plaban Roy (2012): Trade Life Cycle Events,
http://www.coolavenues.com/mba-journal/finance/trade-life-cycle-events?page=0,1
(05.07.2012)

Bremser, Frank / Schäder, Barbara (2012): Alternative Handelsplattformen - Das sind
die jungen Wilden der Börsenwelt, Financial Times Online Edition: March 26, 2012,
http://www.ftd.de/unternehmen/finanzdienstleister/:alternative-handelsplattformen-das-
sind-die-jungen-wilden-der-boersenwelt/70014316.html

Buti, Sabrina / Rindi, Barbara (2008): Hidden Orders and Optimal Submission
Strategies in a Dynamic Limit Order Market, Working Book, December 19, 2008,
http://books.ssrn.com/sol3/books.cfm?abstract_id=1100303 (08.03.2010)

Celent (2008): The Evolution of Direct Market Access (DMA) Trading Services in the US
and Europe, http://www.celent.com/reports/evolution-direct-market-access-dma-trading-
services-us-and-europe

CentralAct (2012): http://www.centralact.com/wissen/begriffe-a-z/

CESR – Committee of European Securities Regulators (2010): Waivers from Pre-trade Transparency Obligations under the Markets in Financial Instruments Directive (MiFID) – Updated, Working Book CESR/09-324, March 9, 2010, http://www.cesr-eu.org/popup2.php?id=5754 (11.03.2010)

Defin.de (2012): http://www.deifin.de/thema008f.htm

Deutsche Börse Group (2009): Xetra Release 10.0 – Marktmodell Aktien, September 21, 2009, http://deutsche-boerse.com/dbag/dispatch/de/binary/gdb_content_pool/imported_files/public_files/10_do wnloads/31_trading_member/10_Products_and_Functionalities/20_Stocks/50_Xetra_M arket_Model/marktmodell_aktien.pdf (11.03.2010)

Deutsche Börse Group (2012): Glossary, http://deutsche-boerse.com/dbg/dispatch/en/kir/dbg_nav/about_us/30_Services/40_Know_how/10_Stoc k_Exchange_A_Z?glossaryWord

Der Aktionär (2009): Milliardengewinne mit Flash Trading. Website of Der Aktionär, 2009. URL: http://www.deraktionaer.de/xist4c/web/Milliardengewinne-mit-Flash-Trading_id_1721__dld_10735419_.htm;jsessionid=D5003F4FEAFB9D53761C21EB1B5 2207E

Domowitz, Ian / Finkelshteyn, Ilya / Yegerman, Henry (2008): Cul de Sacs and Highways – An Optical Tour of Dark Pool Trading Performance, Investment Technology Group (ITG), Working Book, August 2008

European Union (2004): Directive 2004/39/EC of the European Parliament and of the Council f 21 April 2004 on markets in financial instruments, Brussels. URL: http://europa.eu/legislation_summaries/internal_market/single_market_services/financial _services_general_framework/l24036e_en.htm

Financial Services Authority (2005): FSA Handbook on Planning for MiFID, November 2005, http://www.fsa.gov.uk/pubs/international/PLanning_mifid.pdf (05.03.2010)

Financial Times (2012): Trading Room, http://www.ft.com/intl/trading-room (18.08.2012)

Goldstein, Steve (2009): Study: 'Dark Pools' account for 4 % of European Trades, The Wall Street Journal Online Edition: November 2, 2009, http://online.wsj.com/article/SB125715042090622227.html (09.12.2009)

Grant, Jeremy (2009): Trading in European 'dark pools' leaps fivefold since start of year, Financial Times Online Edition: November 2, 2009, http://www.ft.com/intl/cms/s/0/a43d96f0-c74e-11de-bb6f-00144feab49a.html#axzz27TYrw1Zw (01.09.2012)

Grant, Jeremy (2009): Bank dark pools only 1.25 % of Europe trading, Financial Times Online Edition: December 16, 2009, http://www.ft.com/cms/s/0/57423724-ea6d-11de-a9f5-00144feab49a.html (18.12.2009)

Grant, Jeremy (2009): New Nomura dark pool a first, in: Financial Times, 09.12.2009, p. 29

Grant, Jeremy (2009): Regulator research sheds more light on dark pools, in: Financial Times, 18.12.2009, p. 26

InteractiveBrokers.com (2012):
http://www.interactivebrokers.com/en/trading/orders/pegmid.php (03.03.2012)

InteractiveBrokers.de (2012):
http://www.interactivebrokers.de/de/trading/orders/aon.php?ib_entity=de (01.03.2012)

Kisling, Whitney / Westbrook, Jesse (2009): Flash Trade Halt Backed for Nasdaq, Bats as SEC Votes (Update1), Bloomberg.com: September 18, 2009, http://www.bloomberg.com/apps/news?pid=20601087&sid=aCHizjnQq73E (03.03.2010)

Kuls, Norbert (2009): Insiderhandel - Blitzhandel gerät in Amerika unter Beschuss, Frankfurter Allgemeine Online Edition: August 6, 2009, http://www.faz.net/s/RubF3F7C1F630AE4F8D8326AC2A80BDBBDE/Doc~E678F98A6F 3524E99A1A05AC89E54E0C8~ATpl~Ecommon~Scontent.html (18.12.2009)

MarketResearch.com (2009): Securities Brokers Report, December 14, 2009, http://www.marketresearch.com/product/display.asp?productid=2523872&xs=r&SID=73 293553-472507764-410499973&curr=USD (04.03.2010)

Mehta, Nina (2010): Penny Fractions for Stock Quotes May Slow Dark Pools (Update 1), Bloomberg.com, January 26, 2010, http://www.bloomberg.com/apps/news?pid=20601057&sid=a7CfB237M_Ps (04.02.2010)

Private Trader Club (2012): http://www.privatetraderclub.com/index.php/mid,102,/lexikon_letter,/lexikon (16.06.2012)

Ramistella, Alex (2006): Crossing Networks: Bringing Back Large Block Trades to Institutional Trading, The Tower Group, Inc., Needham, MA USA, Reference # V46:11SM, February, 2006

Reuters (2010): US-Börsenaufsicht überprüft Hochfrequenzhandel und Dark Pools. Website of Reuters, 2010. URL: http://de.reuters.com/article/companiesNews/idDEBEE60D02O20100114 (14.01.2010)

Schmerken, Ivy (2010): Algorithmic Trading - Credit Suisse Introduces Block Algos to Tap Liquidity in CrossFinder ATS and Other Venues Simultaneously, Advanced Trading, March 18, 2010, http://www.advancedtrading.com/algorithms/223900065 (10.11.2010)

SEC – U.S. Securities and Exchange Commission (1998): Regulation of Exchanges and Alternative Trading Systems, http://www.sec.gov/rules/final/34-40760.txt (19.12.2009)

SEC – U.S. Securities and Exchange Commission (2000): Regulation of Alternative Trading Systems, http://www.sec.gov/rules/final/34-40760.txt (19.12.2009)

SEC – U.S. Securities and Exchange Commission (2009): Strengthening the Regulation of Dark Pools Fact Sheet – SEC Open Meeting: October 21, 2009, http://www.sec.gov/news/press/2009/2009-223-fs.htm (12.12.2009)

The Economist (2009): High-frequency trading – Rise of the machines. Website of The Economist, 2009. URL: http://www.economist.com/businessfinance/displaystory.cfm?story_id=14133802 (21.09.2009)

The New York Times (2009): Stock Traders Find Speed Pays, in Milliseconds. Charles Duhigg, Website of "The New York Times", 24.07.2009. URL: http://www.nytimes.com/2009/07/24/business/24trading.html (20.09.2009)

Turquoise Homepage: http://www.tradeturquoise.com/tq_about.shtml (08.12.2009)

Wikinvest.com, 2012: http://www.wikinvest.com/wiki/Multilateral_Trading_Facility_(MTF) (07.02.2012)